D0736153

MITCHELL

WHO HAS SEEN THE WIND

NOTES

COLES EDITORIAL BOARD

Bound to stay open

Publisher's Note

Otabind (Ota-bind). This book has been bound using the patented Otabind process. You can open this book at any page, gently run your finger down the spine, and the pages will lie flat.

ABOUT COLES NOTES

COLES NOTES have been an indispensible aid to students on five continents since 1948.

COLES NOTES are available for a wide range of individual literary works. Clear, concise explanations and insights are provided along with interesting interpretations and evaluations.

Proper use of COLES NOTES will allow the student to pay greater attention to lectures and spend less time taking notes. This will result in a broader understanding of the work being studied and will free the student for increased participation in discussions.

COLES NOTES are an invaluable aid for review and exam preparation as well as an invitation to explore different interpretive paths.

COLES NOTES are written by experts in their fields. It should be noted that any literary judgement expressed herein is just that – the judgement of one school of thought. Interpretations that diverge from, or totally disagree with any criticism may be equally valid.

COLES NOTES are designed to supplement the text and are not intended as a substitute for reading the text itself. Use of the NOTES will serve not only to clarify the work being studied, but should enhance the readers enjoyment of the topic.

ISBN 0-7740-3371-1

© COPYRIGHT 1999 AND PUBLISHED BY
COLES PUBLISHING COMPANY
TORONTO—CANADA
PRINTED IN CANADA

Manufactured by Webcom Limited
Cover finish: Webcom's Exclusive **DURACOAT**

CONTENTS

W.O. Mitchell: Brief Biography

W.O. Mitchell was born in Weyburn, Saskatchewan, in 1914. His father, like Brian O'Connal's father in the book, owned and operated a drugstore. Like Brian's father also, W.O. Mitchell's father died when his son was still in boyhood.

Because of health problems, Mitchell was taken to live in Florida, where he completed his high school education. During that time, however, he was a frequent visitor to the Prairies, and he enrolled at the University of Manitoba for his further education. After graduation, he held a variety of jobs and travelled widely in Europe and the United States. At the age of 27, having returned to Canada, he obtained his teaching certificate from the University of Alberta. Afterward, he taught school in a number of small Prairie towns.

Through all the years of travelling and working, he had been writing and, in 1942, his first success came with the publication of a short story in *Maclean's*. In 1948, he became the magazine's fiction editor, a post he held for three years.

Mitchell became a prolific writer, producing work for radio, television and newspapers, as well as several books. *Who Has Seen The Wind*, first published in 1947, was an immediate success. In 1953, with the publication of *The Alien*, Mitchell won the *Maclean's* fiction award.

Mitchell is, above all, a Prairie novelist. He knows the Prairies, and he writes from the life he knows. His radio and television series, "Jake and the Kid," was a delightful, humorous odyssey of life in a small Saskatchewan town. His novel, *The Kite*, again concerns a Prairie boy, Keith MacLean, and his probing of the meaning of existence. That story is enhanced by Daddy Sherry, who is, at the age of 111, the personification of Prairie wisdom. Later, in 1973, the author examined an Alberta Stoney Indian problem involving a love affair between a white Indian agent and an Indian girl.

Who Has Seen The Wind occupies a central place in Mitchell's work. It expresses most charmingly and most incisively two themes that preoccupy his work: the Prairies as a symbol of the eternal, with which man is always troubled; and the small town as a microcosm exposing the passions that motivate man.

1

It is the novel of a man who knows, from experience, the influence exerted by man's closeness to Nature.

Major Works

Who Has Seen The Wind	1947
The Alien	1953
Jake and the Kid	1961
The Kite	1962
The Vanishing Point	1973

Characters in the Novel

Ab: Sean O'Connal's hired man. He is a convert to evangelical religion and, as a result, keeps hiding Sean's pipes and tobacco. He marries Annie.

Abercrombie (Mr.): The town banker. He appears to be as stubborn and narrow-minded as his wife. He refuses Sean's application for a loan to begin an irrigation project.

Abercrombie (Mrs.): The banker's wife. The source of much evil in the town: Mr. Hislop's departure; the mistreatment of the Wongs; the persecution of the Bens.

Abercrombie, (Mariel): The Abercrombies' daughter. She flourishes under the regime of Miss MacDonald, who gives her special tasks to do. She leads the other girls at the school into making the Wong children uncomfortable.

Annie: Sean's housekeeper-cook. She has an ugly cast in her right eye, which Brian helps her to correct with the purchase of spectacles. Only when she throws the spectacles away does Ab ask her to marry him.

Belterlaben, Sammy: This is the real name of "Saint Sammy," the religious fanatic who lives in a piano box on the prairie.

The Bens: The Bens live at Haggerty's Coulee, on the prairie. Mrs. Ben is a slovenly, care-worn woman who does laundry for the townfolk. The Ben is a lazy, drunken man who makes money from digging graves. He makes most of his money, however, from selling moonshine liquor. In order to find a hiding place for his still, the Ben becomes a member of the Presbyterian Church, only to be exposed as a rogue when his still blows up. He is finally jailed, as a result of Mr. Powelly's work, for his illegal activities. The Young Ben is one of the most formative influences in Brian's life: amoral and free, he symbolizes the Prairie.

Bowdage, Mrs.: A churchwoman who delivers a paper on democracy at the parent-teachers meeting.

Briggs, Mr.: The school caretaker. He seems to be an efficient, kindly man. Mr. Digby sometimes goes to his room to smoke.

Candy, Bent: A deacon of the Baptist Church who seems to have success in farming when no one else has. He covets

3

Saint Sammy's Clydesdale horses and builds a new barn to house them, even though he uses tractors on his farm. He buys Magnus Petersen's land in order to evict Sammy.

China Kids: This is the nickname for Tang and Vooie Wong. Tang is shunned by the other girls at school and suffers the misery of planning a birthday party at which none of them show up. The town puts the family on welfare, until Tang is sent to an uncle in Vancouver and Vooie goes to a home in Winnipeg.

Cobb, Mr.: The town plumber. Owner of Cobb's Plumbing Shop.

Digby, James: The school principal. About 38 years old. A sensitive, scholarly man.

The Funders: Mr. Funder, who owns Funder's Meat Market, is one of the Presbyterian elders who refuse to support Mr. Hislop in the dispute over the use of candles in the CGIT service. Charles Funder attends school with Brian. Mrs. Funder has a baby every spring; she has her ninth in Chapter 12.

Gatenby, Allie: One of the Ben's drinking cronies. He joins Joe Pivott in the trick to scare the Ben by pretending to be ghosts.

Geddes, Mrs.: The woman with whom Digby boards.

Gillis, Mr.: The town secretary and the school board secretary.

Harris, Jake: Owner of a hardware store, "a slight, sad little man with thinning hair and a rather narrow face." He sells Mrs. O'Connal the tube skates for Brian. He makes a major contribution at the school board meeting when he is unwilling to have Mr. Digby and Miss Thompson resign. He is also the town policeman.

Hislop, John Hewlitt: The minister of the Presbyterian church before Mr. Powelly. His concern for Romona shows his Christian charity. He has a scholarly turn of mind, but Mrs. Abercrombie objects to his untidy yard. He resigns when the elders refuse to support him in the dispute over the use of candles in the CGIT service. His wife has slightly gray hair, "an intense look," and slightly protruding upper teeth.

The Hoffmans: Mr. Hoffman appears to be a travelling salesman. He seems to be an indulgent father: he gets into enormous difficulties when he allows his son, Forbsie, to keep rabbits; he has pigeons in the barn loft; and he looks after Jappy when Brian has to give up the dog for a while. Forbsie, later nicknamed "Fat," is the first friend Brian meets in the novel, and they are together in a number of episodes.

James, Miss: One of the women with whom Miss Thompson stays. She works in Blaine's Store.

Jaques, Mr.: The town undertaker. An elder in the Presbyterian Church.

Jenkins, Mr.: Owner of a dairy. An elder in the Presbyterian Church.

Johnson, Mr.: Owner of a men's clothing store. A member of the school board.

MacCosham, Elijah: The man who converted Ab to evangelical religion.

MacDonald, Miss: The teacher before Miss Thompson. A harsh disciplinarian, she is confronted by Mrs. O'Connal over her treatment of Brian in the incident about washing his hands. She resigns.

MacKellar, Mr.: The town's railway express agent.

MacMurray, Mrs.: Maggie O'Connal's mother and Brian's grandmother.

Mortimer, Judge: The town magistrate and a member of the school board. He is an ally of Mrs. Abercrombie and Mr. Powelly. Though he is one of the Ben's customers, he sentences the man to jail. He finally rebels at the school board meeting when Mrs. Abercrombie is rude to him, and he proposes the motion to accept her resignation.

Neally, Mr.: The town mayor. He is also the owner of a two-chair barber shop. He is unwilling to relieve the plight of the Wongs, and he resents Miss Thompson's interference in the matter.

The O'Connals: Gerald O'Connal, the town druggist, is married to Maggie. They have two sons, Brian and Bobbie. Bobbie is two years younger than Brian, and his illness at the beginning of the novel causes the family great anxiety.

Palmer, Milt: The town's shoemaker and harnessmaker. One of the really interesting minor characters, he is an uneducated man with a philosophical turn of mind. He exchanges books with Digby, and has long philosophical discussions with the teacher.

Petersen, Magnus: Owner of the land on which Saint Sammy lives. He later sells out to Bent Candy.

Pivott, Joe: The driver of the dray for Sherry's mill, and the owner of 21 Llewellyn setters. He is also the town's practical joker and is responsible for the attempt to scare the Ben by pretending to be a ghost. He is kind to the children, taking them for rides on his dray. It is under the wheels of his dray that the dog, Jappy, dies.

Powelly, Mr.: The minister who succeeds Mr. Hislop. Along with Mrs. Abercrombie, he personifies the malevolent forces in the town. He is responsible for the Ben's imprisonment and tries to have the Young Ben prosecuted for the theft of a gun and ammunition from the hardware store. He is also behind the attempt, at the school board meeting, to have the Young Ben sent away to an institution.

Romona: A "slightly fey derelict" who lives in a shack at the end of First Street. Her habit of entertaining the men who drop off passing freight trains offends Mrs. Abercrombie, who does not want the church to give the woman a Christian hamper. When Mr. Hislop insists, he incurs Mrs. Abercrombie's undying enmity. Romona leaves the town early in the novel.

Sherry, Arthur: One of Brian's friends. Also known as Art and Artie, he is two years older than Brian. He is the boy who mistreats the gopher and is punished by the Young Ben. He is a rather cynical young man.

Spencer, Miss: A teacher in the school.

Stapells, Mr.: The town's mailman.

Stickle, Mr.: A round, little man, the editor of the town newspaper, the *Times*.

Svarich, Peter: The town doctor. A very successful man, he is able to own a Buick and build a new medical building. When practising in Azure, he had become engaged to Ruth Thompson. His shame over his Ukrainian origin causes him to be too self-assertive and demanding. He is, nevertheless, a caring, compassionate man, and he pays the Wongs' grocery bill.

Taylor, Miss: One of the women with whom Miss Thompson stays, she works in the telephone office.

Thompson, Ruth: The teacher who succeeds Miss MacDonald at the town school.

Thorborn, Mr.: Owner of the livery stable and draying business, he is a Presbyterian elder and chairman of the school board. He does not resist Mrs. Abercrombie's evil influence until the fateful meeting of the school board, when he is willing and eager to accept her resignation.

Wong, Mr.: The father of Tang and Vooie, he operates the Bluebird Cafe. After the death of his wife, he becomes despondent, "retired to the tranquillity of his dark kitchen to sit for long, lonely periods of time." He is given the unjustified reputation of being an opium eater. His business declines through neglect and, when his children are taken from him, he hangs himself.

Plot Summary

On a purely narrative level, *Who Has Seen The Wind* is the story of a boy growing up. At the beginning of the book, Brian O'Connal is four years old; at the end, he is almost 11. The years between are an account of the experiences that contribute to his emerging maturity: school, sex education, relatives, the death of a pet dog and the death of his father and grandmother. In that development, the boy's life is strongly influenced by his environment: he grows up in a small town in the midst of the prairie.

On the symbolic level, the novel is, most importantly, a story of spiritual growth. Brian is a sensitive, intelligent boy who responds with feeling to the natural world around him. At first, because of his immaturity, his response is almost purely sensual and innocent. Gradually, however, he links that response with puzzling questions about the meaning of human life. At the end of the book he knows the assurance of the divine element in human existence. He becomes, in a word, mature.

On a second symbolic level, the book exposes the darkness in the heart of man. The small town is no Eden. It is dominated by the malevolent Mrs. Abercrombie and the hypocritical Mr. Powelly. They are simply the most remarkable of the town's wicked citizens. In fact, there is an undercurrent of unfortunate qualities in the population: avarice, bigotry and sheer indifference. That darkness of the human heart contrasts sharply with the decency of people such as the O'Connals, Mr. Digby and Miss Thompson.

Chapter by Chapter
Summaries & Commentaries

NOTE: All quotations are from *Who Has Seen The Wind*, W.O. Mitchell. Macmillan Co. of Canada Ltd., 1960.

PART I • CHAPTER I

Summary

It was June, and the Saskatchewan prairie surrounded the town, waiting for the unfailing wind that would first revive the grasses and, later, in hot gusts, erode the black topsoil.

A single, homesteader's sod hut had established the town in 1875, and now the population was 1,800. Its frame buildings formed avenues with Prairie names—Bison, Riel, Qu'Appelle, Blackfoot, Fort. There were cement sidewalks from First Street to Sixth Street; from there, a boardwalk stretched to the prairie.

At Sixth Street, five houses up from MacTaggart's Corner, stood the vine-covered, three-storied home of the O'Connals. Brian Sean MacMurray O'Connal, the four-year-old son of Gerald, the druggist, and his wife, Maggie, was playing in the breakfast room. Upset at the fuss his baby brother was receiving, he was pretending to be an ant. His play was interrupted by his grandmother, who ordered him to play outside because the baby was ill and should not be disturbed.

Outside, Brian vented his anger on the sand in his sandbox. Suddenly, an unfamiliar face appeared. It was Forbsie Hoffman, who showed Brian the trick of making a pebble hang on the tip of his tongue. When Brian explained that his baby brother was sick and was going to heaven where God lives, Forbsie declared that God lived right in town. Brian immediately wanted to go to God, so that he could punish his grandmother. Forbsie agreed to show him God's house.

The boys walked through the swirling wind of the streets until they reached Knox Presbyterian Church. Forbsie left to go home for supper.

Brian knocked twice at the church door. There was no answer. He assumed that God must be busy in the bathroom. The minister's wife, from the house next door to the church, noticed him. She tried to explain that God was not like people; you could not see Him. She advised Brian to come back next morning, after breakfast, when he could talk to her husband.

As he walked thoughtfully away, Brian suddenly found himself face to face with the open prairie, for the first time in his life. He walked into the hip-deep grass, enchanted by the sights and sounds of prairie life, enjoying the warm wind that blew around him. Again, he was surprised by an unfamiliar face. A barefoot boy appeared before him. Brian asked him if this was his prairie. There was no answer. The boy simply turned and walked away, until he was a mere speck in the distance. The prairie was so beautiful that Brian decided God must like the boy's prairie.

Commentary

Of prime importance in this opening chapter is the naturalness with which Mitchell describes the life of a four-year-old prairie boy. Brian's life and emotions are simple. He is absorbed by childhood games, imagining himself to be an ant, and stepping on the cracks in the pavement. He also experiences childlike emotions: anger at his grandmother because the baby has a blanket tent, while he has not; and innocent delight in the beauty of prairie life. In addition, Mitchell portrays shrewdly the childlike nature of Brian's thoughts, such as when we see the boy's misunderstanding of what God is and where He lives. The simplicity of this portrait of a four-year-old boy is noteworthy.

Of equal importance is the picture of nature that Mitchell paints. The ever-present wind breathes through a landscape that is full of life. On the surface, it appears vast and unmoving. However, among the rustling grasses, a whole, living world moves busily: grasshoppers and gophers, larks and hawks, butterflies and dragonflies. It is a world of wonderment, which Mitchell has re-created with sentences that flow softly and rhythmically.

CHAPTER 2

Summary

In the O'Connal living room, Sean O'Connal, Brian's uncle, sat uncomfortably talking to Brian's grandmother, Mrs.

MacMurray, who was Maggie O'Connal's mother. She was making a "middy" for Brian. Uncle Sean ridiculed the outfit, declaring that a boy should wear overalls. Mrs. MacMurray objected to Sean's criticism and to his language. However, Sean won the verbal battle, and the grandmother retreated angrily. Brian admired his uncle for this victory.

Brian gave his uncle an account of his adventures that afternoon. In reply, Sean told Brian of a little old man who lived on the prairie. It was a humorous account of an Irish leprechaun.

Gerald O'Connal, Brian's father, arrived home. He was unlike his older brother, Sean. Gerald's hair was a darker auburn, and his face was clean-shaven. Whereas Sean had a quick temper, Gerald was almost shy. Though Sean felt protective of his brother, he respected his university education, his business and his family.

Gerald expressed his worry over the baby's condition, and Sean tried to reassure him that everything would be fine. When Gerald asked Sean how he was managing, a change came over the elder brother. The years of drought had bewildered him, as he had had to watch the dry topsoil being blown from the land. Then he had discovered the answer: to save the topsoil, farmers should turn to strip-farming, planting their crops in strips, across the prevailing winds. As he spoke of what needed to be done, he became eloquent and evangelistic. As he followed his grandmother, who was calling him to eat, Brian was spellbound by the power of his uncle's words.

Commentary

The chapter is of interest for its fascinating introduction to Sean O'Connal. He is presented as a man of impressive vitality. His passionate, earthy speech is a mirror of his intense, vigorous nature. He speaks bluntly and directly, a habit that upsets Grandmother MacMurray. Moreover, there is a poetic ingredient in him, seen when he tells Brian the fanciful story about the leprechaun and when he speaks so eloquently and knowingly about the land. It is little wonder that Brian reveres his uncle.

The contrast between the two brothers is also noteworthy. Both were over six feet tall, and both had the O'Connal red hair. However, the similarities ended there. Sean's face was decorated with a large, red mustache, whereas Gerald was clean-shaven. More important, the droughts of the late 1920s and the 1930s had not tamed Sean's quick temper. In contrast, Gerald was a much quieter individual. In addition, unlike Sean, Gerald was a well-educated businessman.

This chapter continues the suspense over the illness of Brian's baby brother. The first chapter emphasized the childlike resentment Brian felt at the attention his brother was receiving. In this chapter, Gerald O'Connal expresses his grave concern over the baby's survival.

CHAPTER 3

Summary
The next day, Brian stood on a chair in the kitchen, watching the morning porridge boil. He thought the bursting bubbles looked like old men's mouths opening and closing.

His father came in, and Brian called to him to come and see the bubbling porridge. Mr. O'Connal, worried about the baby, replied that he did not have time now, and left the house.

Brian decided that the baby was no better. Nobody had come to tuck Brian into bed the previous night. For a long time, he had lain awake, listening to the lonely, frightening sound of the wind against the house. At last he had left his bed and gone down to the second floor. Peeking into his parents' room, he had seen them anxiously tending the baby, who lay in his crib under a tent-blanket. Brian had returned to his bed and fallen asleep, thinking of the boy he had met on the prairie.

The next morning, at breakfast, Brian's grandmother appeared and ordered him down from the chair. She was going to be bossy again today, Brian thought. As he ate his porridge, he imagined God eating His porridge, with a bowl as big as the prairie and the milk squirting from a long hose. Mrs. MacMurray ordered Brian out of the house, warning him not to return until noon. She was worried about the baby, who seemed to be dying.

Brian went to visit Mr. Hislop, the minister, who took him to visit the church sanctuary. Mr. Hislop explained to Brian that God looked after everything: flowers, trees, birds and people. Brian asked if God looked after the prairie boy, too, because he wanted to be like that boy, who did not live in a house and had the prairie wind in his hair. Mr. Hislop agreed that God looked after the prairie boy. After the minister had told him about angels, Brian left.

After Brian's departure, Mr. Hislop returned to mowing his back lawn. He was distressed at the untidy condition of his yard, which had been criticized by one of his congregation, Mrs. Abercrombie. His differences with Mrs. Abercrombie had begun with Romona, who had lived in a shack at the end of First Street. She was a derelict who lived on scraps from the cafe and the meat market. Mrs. Abercrombie resented Romona because she welcomed to her shack the hungry men who dropped off the freight trains that passed through town. Thus, her washing line was often filled with men's clothing. Romona also infuriated Mrs. Abercrombie by decorating the windows of her shack at Christmas, with red tissue paper, which Mrs. Abercrombie regarded as immoral. One Christmas, Mrs. Abercrombie decided that Romona should not be given one of the church hampers of food distributed to the needy. In spite of Mr. Hislop's pleas, Romona had refused to remove the red tissue paper. But, at Mr. Hislop's insistence, she had still been given the hamper. Even though Romona had left town the following spring, Mrs. Abercrombie still smarted from her defeat. And now, though the yard was still embarrassingly untidy, Mr. Hislop became lost in philosophical thought.

Several blocks away, Brian sat on a fence with Forbsie Hoffman. Still thinking of angels with their wings of feathers, Brian declared that he wanted to get a pillow, so that both Forbsie and he could make feather wings. He entered the house without being caught by his grandmother and came out with a pillow, a paring knife and some string. While they were struggling to make wings out of the small feathers, Arthur Sherry, "a six-year-old cynic," arrived. He poured scorn on their project, pointing out that real wings were made out of feathers that grew. Brian protested, though he began to feel that the plan was doomed. When Arthur returned home to eat, Brian was left staring at the feathers, knowing now that Arthur was right.

Commentary

The beginning of the chapter portrays well the bewilderment of a four-year-old who is suddenly not receiving the care and attention to which he has been accustomed. The illness of the baby dominates the O'Connal household and claims the energies of the adults. As a result, Brian is lonely and confused.

The brief portrait of Mr. Hislop is a delightful cameo of the minister. He is obviously a sincere, compassionate man, worthy of his position as a leader of his flock. He endures Mrs. Abercrombie's anger over Romona and is so strong in his convictions that his point of view is triumphant. He is clearly so committed to his faith that, when he feels principles are at stake, he can display courage and tenacity. However, the portrait has aspects of humor. Mr. Hislop is not a man who manages very well in the practical, everyday world. Mrs. Abercrombie is right, his yard is a mess. Faced with the task of cleaning it up, though, Mr. Hislop loses himself in the pleasure of philosophical thoughts.

There are many delightful moments in the novel, in which Mitchell re-creates shrewdly the thoughts and fantasies that preoccupy the minds of small children. The incident involving the pillow is one of those moments. The picture of the boys, sneezing as the tiny feathers swirl around them, struggling manfully to master their elusive materials, is both hilarious and heart-warming.

CHAPTER 4

Summary
Under the shade of the poplars in the minister's garden, Mr. Hislop and Mr. Digby, the school principal, were talking.

In spite of his lack of money, Mr. Digby was a satisfied man, looking forward to his summer holiday.

The two men were discussing moral laws and values. The minister declared that the foundation of values existed with Plato and Christ, long ago, and that it all found its source in God. Mr. Digby presented the view shared by his friend, Milt Palmer, the town shoe and harness maker, that moral law and conventions were just "blocks" that men played with.

Their discussion led them to the topic of the Ben family. The Ben father, referred to as the Ben, had "about as much moral conscience as the prairie wind." Young Ben, it was

14

observed, seemed to be no different. He had begun attending school a year late, when forced to do so by the school board. Before coming to school, the boy had never entered the town. When he had travelled with his father from Haggerty's Coulee, where they lived, he had sat on the prairie at the edge of town, simply watching. He had been seen at other times wearing very little clothing, running across the prairie.

Mr. Hislop broke off the discussion, saying that he had to get his lawn mowed. As he began the work, he was warmed by the memory of Brian's visit to see him.

Lying on the floor of his home, Brian stared at the white paper in front of him. He was going to draw. He could not go out to play with Forbsie, because Forbsie had the mumps. He could not play with Arthur Sherry, because Arthur was waiting outside to wrestle him down. He began to draw God, using a variety of colors. Then he surrounded that figure with a number of smaller, spiderlike Gods. Engrossed in his project, he imagined himself talking to God, who called himself R.W. God and promised to punish Brian's grandmother and Arthur Sherry. Brian answered that his grandmother wasn't so bad now that the baby was better, but he was pleased at God's promise to kick Arthur Sherry. Brian's fantasy ended with his mother's arrival.

At dinner that night, the baby joined the family at the table for the first time since his illness. Like all babies, he was messy with his food and, just learning to talk, mimicked the words of the adults around him.

After breakfast the next day, Brian hurried out to play, taking with him his picture of God. He laid the drawing carefully on a poplar leaf and made up a song about Him. This drawing of a little man was Brian's R.W. God. When his father said "Amen" at the end of mealtime grace, Brian began to add "R.W."

Unfortunately for Brian, his mother appeared on the scene just as R.W. God belched. When Brian insisted that he had not belched and that R.W. had done so, Mrs. O'Connal became angry and sent Brian to his room. In his room, Brian told his father all about R.W. God. Mr. O'Connal tried to explain how wrong Brian's thoughts about God were. When Brian said his prayers, he added a blessing for the boy on the prairie and still ended with, "Amen, R.W."

Commentary

This chapter gives insight into the domestic life of the O'Connals. They are obviously a closely knit family. Grandmother MacMurray is a caring lady, who does housework and sews clothes for Brian. Mr. O'Connal, though a big man, is a gentle, indulgent father, who often looks to his wife when the family needs sterner discipline. Mrs. O'Connal, as careful of her speech and manners as Mrs. MacMurray, is an attentive mother, very much concerned about raising Brian properly.

Brian's fantasies about God are as interesting as they are original. It is, of course, amusing to imagine his picture of God, knee-high and riding a vacuum cleaner. Yet the childlike logic behind the fantasies is convincing. For example, Brian gives God the initials "R.W." because, in his world, all important people are addressed by two initials, like Judge E.L. Mortimer. The reasoning is sound, then, even though the conclusion is not. That is the element that makes the fantasies convincing; they are appropriate for a young child.

In this chapter also, W.O. Mitchell communicates subtly and shrewdly some of the flavor of small-town life. This feat is not accomplished by a lengthy description. Instead, it is communicated by means of the simple conversation between Mr. Hislop and Mr. Digby. For example, both men are seen to be concerned about simple, human things. Mr. Hislop wants to get his lawn mowed before he meets Mrs. Abercrombie again on Sunday. His discussion of moral law is not philosophical or intellectual. To him, it is a fundamental fact of experience that God is the foundation of moral law. Mr. Digby is a contented man, as long as he has tobacco for his pipe and time for a conversation with his friend. Life in the town seems to take its cue from the rhythms of nature; the tension, bustle and competitiveness of the city are far distant.

CHAPTER 5

Summary

Brian had a puppy, a fox terrier given to him by his father.

Mr. O'Connal wanted him to have a friend to play with, instead of talking to R.W. Brian, Forbsie and Artie took great delight in the new pet, but Grandmother MacMurray was not at all pleased. She complained that it was smelly and that it yapped too much. She also complained that it chewed things, and that its tugging at her skirts made walking dangerous, because she wore a brace on her leg. Finally, when grandmother declared that the dog was giving her nervous indigestion, Mrs. O'Connal decided that the animal must not enter the house and must sleep in the garage. That night, when his parents had gone to visit the Abercrombies to play bridge, Brian, restless and lonely, sneaked out to the garage to sleep with his puppy.

At the Abercrombies, both of the O'Connals were pre-occupied as they played bridge. Gerald's mind was on his visit that afternoon to the doctor's office. Dr. Svarich had told Mr. O'Connal that he was suffering from gastritis, which might turn into an ulcer. The druggist was advised to relax more and to take up a game, such as golf. Mrs. O'Connal worried constantly about her two sons, hoping that her mother would wake up if the baby cried.

The Abercrombies had their own concerns. Mr. Abercrombie, the bank manager, spoke of the financial problems of the West. There were, he declared, three causes of the present difficulties: too much credit, the wastefulness of the farmers and too much concentration on agriculture. In contrast, Mrs. Abercrombie could think only of what she regarded as problems at the church. The church, she exclaimed, needed a different minister, one more vigorous than Mr. Hislop.

After the O'Connals returned home, trouble arose. Brian was missing. Jake Harris, the town's garbage collector, fireman and policeman, was summoned to find the boy. Jake discovered him asleep in the garage with his puppy. Mr. O'Connal treated the matter seriously. He reminded Brian that the dog had been obtained against the wishes of Brian's mother. If there was any more trouble with it, the dog would have to go.

Commentary

The chapter gives a clear indication of the importance of social status in a small town. Mr. and Mrs. Abercrombie are people of consequence. Mr. Abercrombie is the bank manager.

However, his wife is the more imposing figure. A large, shapeless woman, she wears three rings on her fingers: one that had belonged to her mother, a large solitaire that had marked her husband's promotion to bank manager and a third she had received on giving birth to her daughter, Mariel. She is also an active woman in the town, working with the church, the Red Cross, the Imperial Order of the Daughters of the Empire, the Eastern Star, the library board and the local relief committee for the poor. Because of her insensitivity, she dominates all of the committees on which she serves. Proud of her expensive rings, secure in the prestige of her husband's position and vain over the trip they had taken to Europe six years earlier, Mrs. Abercrombie is an impressive social force.

CHAPTER 6

Summary

Mr. Hislop was upset. He had received a letter, signed by Mrs. Abercrombie, from the Ladies' Auxiliary. The women were complaining about the service he had held for the Canadian Girls in Training. It had been a candlelight service, and the women regarded the use of candles as being too Roman Catholic. The minister's despair was caused by the evil influence that Mrs. Abercrombie obviously exerted in the town. She was bitterly intolerant. Earlier, she had objected to his playing tennis with the priest, Father Cochran, and to his combining summer services with the Baptist Church. Consequently, Mr. Hislop felt the uselessness of his task in preaching week after week to Mrs. Abercrombie and to the people who listened to her. At this moment, he longed for the peacefulness and friendliness of his former parish in the Peace River country. He decided to call a meeting of his church elders to discuss the letter and to talk with his friend, Digby.

Brian O'Connal, carrying his puppy, was making his way to the Hoffmans' house. The puppy had been in trouble again. It had pulled down his grandmother's washing line, with the clean clothes on it. As a result, Mr. O'Connal, pressed by Grandmother MacMurray, had declared that the dog had to stay with the Hoffmans until it grew up a little. They had no grandmother to be bothered by it. On the way, Brian met

Forbsie, who was not as interested in the dog as he was in the pigeon he had at home. It had laid eggs, an event that greatly excited Forbsie. Mrs. Hoffman took Brian's puppy, and assured him that it would be allowed to sleep in the house by the stove. Brian played with the puppy all that morning and afternoon. After dinner, he sat in the cellar at home, lonely for his dog.

Mr. Hislop held the meeting with his elders: Judge Mortimer, Mr. Funder, Mr. Nightingale, Mr. Thorborn, Mr. Jaques and Mr. Jenkins. They listened uncomfortably to Mrs. Abercrombie's letter. Judge Mortimer, an ignorant man, was first to speak. He agreed with what the letter said. The rest, except for Mr. Nightingale, who was too deaf to have heard all of the letter, agreed. Mr. Hislop was stunned by their attitude.

Brian spent his mornings and afternoons at the Hoffmans' and gradually came to accept his loss of the puppy. When the pigeon's eggs hatched a week later, Brian and Forbsie were greatly intrigued by the mystery of the origin of the pigeons. Mr. O'Connal explained that the father pigeon had built each egg around each baby pigeon. It rained for the next three days, and Brian was forbidden to visit his puppy. Bored and restless, he thought of replacing his dog with one of Forbsie's baby pigeons.

Mr. Hislop was discussing his problem with Digby. The minister declared that he would have to resign. Digby dismissed that suggestion. The minister, he insisted, was being too sensitive. He should fight back. When Mr. Hislop explained how foolish he felt, Digby tried to console his friend.

Though it was still raining, Brian was in the Hoffmans' loft. He took hold of a baby pigeon gently and stuffed it inside his shirt. He had a replacement for his dog.

Commentary

Mr. Hislop's problem with the Ladies' Auxiliary gives a vivid indication of the narrowness of mind and bigotry that can exist in a small town. The issue is petty: whether the use of candles in a service is against Presbyterian practice. But Mrs. Abercrombie, a busybody, dislikes Mr. Hislop, and she is able to marshal the Auxiliary and the elders against the minister. Idealist that he is, his prime reaction is one of disappointment.

He had not expected such bitterness from his flock. Thus, though the incident itself is minor, its appearance is not. Mr. Hislop's beliefs and his tolerant humanity have been questioned. It presents a genuine crisis for a man who wishes to be a shepherd to his flock.

Brian's daily existence at this point is worthy of attention. The details Mitchell gives us are natural and convincing. Like all small boys, Brian is absorbed by his ownership of a puppy. His sense of loss when the dog is sent to the Hoffmans is not overstated; rather, it is communicated with feeling. The writer also communicates shrewdly and convincingly an aspect of a child's life that adults often overlook: loneliness. Brian has a fine, solid family. His father cares deeply about Brian, his mother is devoted to her sons and Grandmother MacMurray's ceaseless work is a major contribution to the household. Yet Brian's world sometimes seems to exist apart from the world of the adults around him. Thus, he is left to deal in his own way with the feelings prompted by the loss of his dog. He feels lonely, and taking the baby pigeon is his childish way of dealing with those feelings.

CHAPTER 7

Summary

The rain had stopped. Sean O'Connal looked out over his brown, wilted wheat crop and cursed the rain that had come too late to be of benefit.

In his study, Mr. Hislop read over his letter of resignation.

On the back porch of their home, Mr. O'Connal and Brian stared at Brian's baby pigeon, which lay dead. Brian was puzzled by the mystery of death. His father explained that they would now have to bury the bird. Brian insisted that the pigeon be buried on the prairie, away from houses, where the prairie boy lived. As Mr. O'Connal was digging a hole for the bird, the prairie boy appeared briefly among the bushes. Mr. O'Connal told Brian that the boy was the Young Ben. Brian replied that the prairie belonged to the boy, because he lay on it.

Two days later, in fulfilment of Mr. O'Connal's promise, Brian had his puppy back. He lay under the hedge at the side of the house, cradling his dog in his arms. In his contentment, the boy was alive to the sights and sounds of nature around him.

As the day wore on, the wind drifted through the streets and out to the prairie. The shadows lengthened, and the dusk bathed the world in a mellow light.

Commentary

As Part I of the novel draws to a close, it is clear that Brian's life, though simple, is rich in experience. He has had to deal with the tension that grips a household when illness strikes. He has witnessed the grave concern of his father over the baby's sickness, the anxiety of his mother and the irritated bustle of his grandmother. He has also learned something of the weight of responsibility, with which even a child must cope. As tenderly as he might have cared for his puppy, he had to suffer the agonies of losing him for a time, because the dog was annoying the household. Just as important, Brian has had his first encounter with the death of something, the baby pigeon, that was precious to him. The experiences are simple, but they are fundamental. They are part of the experiences that all human beings must know. They are elemental experiences, into which man is initiated early.

Part I closes, as it began, with a sense of the timelessness of the natural world. Chapter 1 began with "the least common denominator of nature," the prairie. It surrounded the town almost silently, vast and shimmering in the June sun. Chapter 7 gives a haunting picture of the natural world, which, with its subdued light and softness, seems to give man and his things—stooks, fences and horses—a clarity they had not possessed during the day's activities. This timeless natural world appears to offer, in the first part of the novel, a sharp and vivid contrast with the world of man. Man, it seems to suggest, is frantic and anxious in his pursuits. He is beset by crises, large and small; illness, farming problems, money worries, a puppy's playfulness and a woman's malevolence. The town, however small, is a center of anxiety. In contrast, the prairie is a place of beauty and grandeur, alive with sights and sounds that delight the boy. It is, indeed, the place of freedom, a fitting kingdom for the Young Ben, who roams its spaces without hindrance.

PART II • CHAPTER 8

Summary

Two years had passed, and it was now the fall of 1931. The wind had eroded more of the black topsoil from the fields, and the crop was poor. But harvest time was still a time of excitement for the town. Farm machinery and equipment went up and down the streets, and long grain freights blocked First Street with their slow progress. Strangers left the trains, looking for work at a dollar and a half a day. The wheat cost 30 cents a bushel to grow and was sold for only 25 cents a bushel, but it had to be harvested.

On the first day of September, Brian awoke. This was to be his first day at school. Now six, he was eager to attend school, just as Artie did already. His dog, Jappy, woke up to greet him, as did his brother, Bobbie.

In the kitchen, trying to hide his excitement, Brian greeted his mother. Mrs. O'Connal's eyes wore a look of concern. She wanted to accompany her son to school, but Brian pointed out that Forbsie was also starting school, and he was going by himself. As he fed his dog, Brian wished that his parents would not be so tense about his starting school. At 8:30, to the accompaniment of tears from his mother, Brian left for school. Mr. O'Connal teased his wife for her sentimentality.

Approaching the school, Brian saw the Wong children, Tang and her brother, Vooie. Mr. Wong ran the Bluebird Cafe. He cooked meals for his children, but left Tang to tend to her brother. As they neared the schoolyard, Artie tried to frighten Brian and Forbsie with stories of the fearsome Miss MacDonald, who was to be their teacher.

When the school bell rang, the children who had been to school before formed two lines, one for boys and one for girls. Miss MacDonald rounded up the newcomers. Inside, she told the beginners to play quietly with plasticine and then handed out the readers to the Grade 3 pupils, of which Artie was one.

Brian quickly felt disappointment and decided to get up and talk to Artie, who sat two rows away. Immediately, Miss MacDonald ordered him to sit down. Brian was confused. He was not doing any harm. Anyway, he thought, the teacher was not his mother. Again, he was ordered to sit down. When he did not do so, Miss MacDonald approached him. As she came near, Brian fingered the water pistol that he had brought to school. When the teacher reached out to guide him back to his seat, he pointed the pistol at her and pulled the trigger. The front of her dress drenched, Miss MacDonald was furious. She hurried him to the principal's office to see Mr. Digby. Brian was not talkative, and Digby had great trouble in impressing upon him that rules must be obeyed.

When Brian had left, Mr. Digby pondered his perennial problem, the Young Ben. As usual, the boy had not shown up for registration. The problem seemed insoluble. The boy's father was an irresponsible drunk who broke all laws and conventions. Mr. Digby decided that he would call on the Bens after lunch.

Commentary

The picture of the economic depression of the Prairies is worth noting. In Chapter 2, Sean O'Connal gave some indications of the problems, when he spoke of the carelessness of the farmers in using land that was being eroded by the ceaseless winds. In this chapter, two years later, even more of the rich topsoil has piled up against fences and buildings. The rain, coming too late, has not alleviated the problem. The wheat crop is poor, and it is being sold at less than it cost to grow. The scenario is rendered even more grim by the sight of the drifting laborers, only half of whom can find employment, jumping from the trains that pass through the town.

The account of Brian's first day of school is both amusing and sad. He was eager to attend school, which is a mark of his growing up. He is also an obedient, sensitive boy. However, his naïvete swiftly brought him into conflict with Miss MacDonald. Mr. Digby clearly emerges as the wiser, more humane character in the drama. He is obviously a compassionate man, with a genuine interest in the children he teaches.

CHAPTER 9

Summary

Straight from school, Brian went to his father's drugstore.

His father's clerk, Leon, was serving Mrs. Abercrombie. Feeling pride in his father's store, Brian went into the dispensary.

Mr. O'Connal was working on a prescription. Brian burst out with an account of what had happened at school. His father's response was calm: Brian would have to make sure that nothing like that happened again: Mr. O'Connal also agreed to be the one to break the news to Mrs. O'Connal. Relieved, Brian left the store. Bobbie and he both recognized their father's indulgence. Their mother was different. She had high expectations of her sons and demanded mature behavior.

Brian was looking, at his father's request, for Bobbie. He was, at that moment, down at the station, watching the express agent, Mr. MacKellar, and two helpers unload the mail from the train that had just come in. During the summer, Bobbie toured the town in his little red wagon. He visited the pool hall, the post office and the town hall. He also dropped in on Mr. Stickle, to watch the presses printing the *Times*. As Bobbie entered the double doors beside the town secretary's office, the bell rang for the daily fire drill. Watching the fire horses in their noon drill was Bobbie's greatest pleasure. Just then, Brian arrived to take Bobbie home.

Mr. Abercrombie's bank was the most pretentious building in town. Inside, Sean O'Connal was trying to raise a loan of $300. Mr. Abercrombie refused flatly. Sean, he insisted, had no security, owed the bank too much already and had an impractical idea. Mr. O'Connal, who wanted the money for an experiment in irrigation, denounced Mr. Abercrombie angrily.

At home, Mrs. O'Connal tied Bobbie in the backyard so that he would not wander away. She then tackled Brian about school, explaining that she wanted him to learn whatever there was to learn. She spoke with such unusual emotion that Brian promised earnestly to do what she wanted.

Mr. Digby walked to Haggerty's Coulee to visit the Bens. As he walked, he thought of the many strappings he had given the Young Ben, largely because the townspeople expected him to whip the boy. As the principal approached the weather-beaten Ben buildings, Mrs. Ben emerged. She did not know where the Young Ben was, but she promised to send him to school the next day, though she could not guarantee that he would get there. She informed Digby that Mr. Ben had been at the cemetery, because somebody had died. It was no use bothering him on a "grave" day, she declared. From information passed on by Mr. Briggs, the school janitor, the teacher knew that there was no point in bothering with the Ben today. If he had dug a grave, he would be in the beer parlor, drinking the money he had earned. Walking home, Digby thought of his friend, Mr. Hislop, who had left the town two years earlier. Digby wondered what moral measurement Hislop would use with the Bens. It was really a hopeless cause, he decided.

In the beer parlor, the Ben was drinking with Mr. Cobb, the plumber, Allie Gatenby and Joe Pivott. With a 50-pound sack of chicken feed resting on his head, the Ben was boasting about the number of illegitimate children he had fathered, declaring there were 133 from coast to coast. That number, he continued, did not include the Young Ben. The Young Ben was, as he had often said before, born fully grown. Joe Pivott asked whether Mrs. Ben knew about all the illegitimate children. The Ben replied firmly that she did not, for he was afraid of only two things: his wife and ghosts. When the Ben left to go to the Bluebird Cafe, Joe Pivott, who was the town's practical joker, decided to play a trick on the Ben.

Hours later, staggering home drunkenly, the Ben was met by two white figures that came threateningly toward him. They were Joe Pivott and Allie Gatenby, dressed in sheets. However, the Ben surprised them. Instead of retreating, he raised his fists and invited them to fight.

Commentary

The chapter emphasizes the character contrast between Gerald O'Connal and his wife. The father is obviously a rather indulgent man who does not like to apply stern discipline to his sons. Thus, Brian is more willing to confess his misdeeds to his father than to face the displeasure of his mother. Mrs. O'Connal takes motherhood seriously. She has an unyielding sense of what is acceptable and unacceptable in the conduct of her sons.

In addition, the brief interview between Mr. Abercrombie and Sean O'Connal delineates the sharp differences between the two men. The banker is a pompous, cautious man, with insufficient imagination to grasp the possibilities of the irrigation experiment proposed by the other. The farmer is the same passionate, evangelistic man who spoke so eloquently in Chapter 2 of ways of solving prairie farming problems.

This chapter also gives more information about the Bens. They are, indeed, a problem. The Ben himself is a drunk who has no concept of the responsibilities of family life. His wife is a weak, harassed woman. The Young Ben is left to his own devices and has become a wild figure, roaming the prairie. The episodes in the tavern and later, involving the Ben and his cronies, are typical village humor. It recalls some of the humorous incidents in the novels of Thomas Hardy.

CHAPTER 10

Summary

On the second day, the Young Ben came to school. Barefoot and gangly, he sat across the aisle from Brian. He could not read, and he did not write. He simply sprawled in his desk and looked out at the prairie. Brian did not talk to the 10-year-old Ben, who was spending his third year in Grade 1, but there seemed to be some kind of bond between the two boys. That bond became evident one morning in January.

The first few months of school had gone well for Brian. In spite of the continuing slight tension between Miss MacDonald and him, he had quickly adapted to the rules of school life. Miss MacDonald had divided the children into three groups: the Gophers, the Ants and the Grasshoppers. Brian was proud to belong to the Gophers, for they were leaders in health, which involved sleeping with the window open, chewing food properly, brushing teeth regularly and washing hands and face before coming to school. But Brian made a mistake. One morning in January, he left home without washing his hands and face. When the teacher asked those who had washed to put up their hands, Brian, out of habit, put up his hand. Miss MacDonald declared that he had told a lie. As a result, Brian was forced to stand in front of the class, with his arms stretched out, the palms of his hands facing the class. He had to stand there all during Grade 1 reading and Grade 3 arithmetic. He was hot and dizzy and his arms ached. The teacher wanted to find some way of ending the punishment, but she could not. She wanted to see tears, as a sign of repentance. The other children watched, grinning, except for the Young Ben, who seemed to become more and more resentful of Brian's punishment. At last Miss MacDonald told Brian to sit down. As he walked to his seat, however, he fainted. Alarmed, the teacher went to him. She was stopped by the Young Ben, who picked Brian up and placed him in his seat. When Brian walked home alone at noon, the Young Ben walked with him, an arm around Brian's waist.

That night, not having confessed his lie to his mother, Brian had difficulty getting to sleep. He was troubled by Miss MacDonald's threat that God punished liars. When he did sleep, he was haunted by a nightmare of God's punishing presence. He awoke screaming. Mrs. O'Connal came to comfort her son, who told her what had happened at school. After Brian had fallen asleep again, she lay awake for a long time.

Two days later, Mrs. O'Connal had an interview with Miss MacDonald. Brian had had to stay away from school, so upset had he been. In her own quiet way, Brian's mother upbraided the teacher for what she had done. Mrs. O'Connal pointed out how important it was that a teacher should like children. She bluntly observed that Miss MacDonald had no right to threaten Brian with God's punishment. She ended by declaring that the teacher must be an unhappy woman, who would be a better, happier teacher were she to have a child of her own.

Commentary

In this chapter, the warm, human aspect of Mrs. O'Connal's character emerges strongly. She shows herself to be a loving, caring parent who understands the complexities and tribulations that six-year-old Brian experiences. She clearly understands very well the terror that adult threats can introduce into a child's life. In this, she is a complete contrast to Miss MacDonald. The teacher is an unbending disciplinarian, who enjoys the power she wields in the classroom. Such is her consciousness of her position that she seems to see the children as potential threats.

The strange alliance between Brian and the Young Ben is forged in this chapter. It is, quite obviously, an unlikely alliance. Brian is the son of a solid citizen, a professional man, and is well-trained in the middle-class virtues of honesty, obedience and cleanliness. The Young Ben is a wild and free spirit, neglected by his parents and shunned by the community. Yet it was Brian's plight that caused the remote Young Ben to become involved in an environment that he had previously ignored.

CHAPTER 11

Summary

The O'Connal family sat in front of the fireplace. Grandmother MacMurray was dozing in her chair. Bobbie was asleep in his father's lap. Brian asked why people slept. His father replied that sleeping was just a habit. Mr. O'Connal went on to remark that he had seen the Young Ben hanging around in front of the house. Brian assured his parents that the boy only wanted to make sure that Brian was all right. Mr. O'Connal suggested that the Young Ben was not a suitable friend, but his wife thought that the friendship was all right. When Brian ventured to ask whether God slept, Mr. O'Connal suggested that it was time for them all to go to bed. They left grandmother sitting alone.

In the darkened room, Grandmother MacMurray's mind gave way to her memories of her dead husband, John, and their early life together. At last she rose and went to bed.

In her room, Mrs. O'Connal prayed earnestly that her sons would turn out well. As she listened to her husband stoking the furnace below, she decided that she would be satisfied if they turned out to be as good as their father.

Shovelling coal into the furnace, Gerald O'Connal thought of Brian. He wondered how the boy had come to question whether God slept. He also wondered at his boy's friendship with the Young Ben.

Mr. O'Connal was pleased at the understanding that seemed to exist between Bobbie and Brian. He hoped that that understanding would last as long as it had between himself and his own brother, Sean. Sean had sent him money to Toronto for his pharmacy course. The money was now paid back and had helped Sean through the years of drought. Mr. O'Connal thought that he should tell Sean that a small sum was still outstanding. His brother could use it to finance his irrigation project. Sean was so careless about money that he would never know the difference.

Commentary
The chapter unfolds at a leisurely pace. This section is almost entirely concerned with the interior thoughts of the adult O'Connals. Consequently, it adds a necessary context to the story of the unfolding life of young Brian. We see his parents as devoted family people. Mrs. O'Connal watches over her young offspring carefully, seeking to guide their footsteps in the way of solid manhood. Mr. O'Connal cherishes his relationship with his brother and sees the strength of that relationship as a desirable goal for his own sons. Together, the husband and wife provide a secure, loving environment in which the two young boys can come to understand the challenges of life.

CHAPTER 12

Summary
Spring came suddenly to the Prairies. The snow melted. The farmers planted their seeding.

In town, there were various signs of awakening. Mariel Abercrombie brought the first crocus to school, and Forbsie saw the first gopher. Mrs. Funder had her ninth spring baby. Mrs. Abercrombie and the new minister, Mr. Powelly, began a campaign of religious visitation. These two were congenial, because Mr. Powelly was just as intolerant as Mrs. Abercrombie.

The Young Ben stayed away from school for three weeks. Miss MacDonald, remembering his defence of Brian, did not report his absence until the second week. She was becoming increasingly nervous of the children and was sure that she needed to change schools.

The Ben always operated a rough still to brew liquor. That spring, he moved it from its hiding place on the prairie and placed it in his well. Unfortunately, the mash boiled over, and several of his livestock became intoxicated. The still would have to be moved again. The Ben was also plagued by money problems. Since the trick played on him by Allie Gatenby and Joe Pivott, he had not dug any graves, claiming that his rheumatism bothered him. He needed money for his beer, his chewing tobacco and his still. Consequently, he began to take and sell eggs without his wife's knowing. That scheme came to an end a month later, when Mrs. Ben caught him and threatened him with the police.

However, the Ben found a solution to his problems. Barney Hepworth, the janitor at the Presbyterian church, died of pneumonia. Immediately, the Ben approached the minister and declared a new-found religious faith. Mr. Powelly welcomed the Ben enthusiastically. He was made church janitor, and the date for his admission to the congregation was set. A week later, he moved his still into the church basement; he had found the ideal hiding place.

The day of the Ben's reception into the congregation was memorable for Brian, too. He awoke early and, as on Sunday mornings, polished the shoes of the family. When he had finished that chore, he wandered out of the house. His attention was caught by the new, delicate leaves of the spirea that were washed with morning dew. As he gazed at a leaf, he was filled with a sense of enchantment. It was a special spell of feeling, broken only by the call of his father to breakfast.

At breakfast, Bobbie and Brian grumbled about the lumpy porridge. It was lumpy every Sunday, because Mr. O'Connal made it. Brian and his father took breakfast up to Mrs. O'Connal. Her breakfast in bed was also part of the Sunday ritual. While she was eating, Mr. O'Connal mentioned that Sean was coming over after church to have dinner with them. Brian was excited at that news, but Mrs. O'Connal found it difficult to be as enthusiastic. Sean's quick generosity, like that of his brother, worried her, as did the language he used.

On his way to church with his family, Brian was hoping that he could recapture the feeling of enchantment he had experienced when he had gazed at the spirea leaf. Inside the church, he looked over the rest of the congregation with interest: Mr. Harris, with the fat, pink neck; the Wong children, whose father never came to church. And then he saw, with excitement, that the Ben and the Young Ben were there. When the congregation rose to sing the first hymn, "Holy, Holy, Holy," Brian did recapture his moment of enchantment. The raindrop on the pebble, he realized, had given him a holy feel-

30

ing. Then, after Mr. Powelly had read Bible passages telling of lost sheep, the Ben was asked to step forward to be received into the congregation. Unfortunately, he did not know that he would be required to shake hands with the minister, and he still had a wad of chewing tobacco hidden in his palm.

Commentary

Brian's moment of enchantment is worth noting since it underlines the responsive, sensitive nature of the boy. He has already, in Chapter 1, responded to the poetry of the prairie, held spellbound by the bustling life of the creatures that inhabit the rustling grasses. In Chapter 12, he has what can be described as a moment of epiphany, a moment of vision. In the beauty of the glistening waterdrop on the spirea leaf, he becomes enchanted by a vision of the holiness of all things. In his own immature way, he comes to realize in church that his precious moment with the leaf was just as religious as the worship offered by the congregation.

Of major interest in this chapter is, of course, the Ben and his cunning activities. He is such an obvious rogue that his antics are as hilarious as they are ingenious. All of his energies are directed toward satisfying his desire for his creature comforts: beer, tobacco and the operation of his still. He will go to any lengths to satisfy those desires. Now he has made a show of becoming respectable, but the conversion can hardly be expected to be lasting.

CHAPTER 13

Summary

When the family returned from church, Sean was already at the house. He impressed the boys, as no other adult did, with his size, his booming voice and his eloquent swearing.

Sean was angry because of his hired man, Ab, who had gone through a religious conversion. As a result, he had tried to cure Sean of drinking and had hidden Sean's pipes and tobacco. Now, Sean cursed, long and loud, about the change that had come over Ab, and he wished he could get his hands on Elijah MacCosham, who had been responsible for Ab's conversion. Soon, however, the conversation of Bobbie and Brian had Sean roaring with laughter, but the boys were sent out to play when their uncle's cursing was mimicked by Bobbie.

By dinnertime, Sean had become quieter. He loved his food, and both Mrs. O'Connal and her mother were good cooks.

After dinner, Sean spoke enthusiastically of the skill of his new cook, Annie. The only trouble with her, he declared, was that she was too fond of Ab. Sean also spoke with great excitement of his irrigation project. His garden, he insisted, would be green and beautiful. He added, however, that if it weren't for his garden, he would think of moving in with Saint Sammy. That was his name for Sammy Belterlaben, who now lived in a piano box on Magnus Petersen's place. Sammy has wonderful Clydesdale horses, to which he has given Biblical names. The horses are the envy of Bent Candy, the Baptist deacon, who had farmed his land successfully, even in the bad years. Thoughts of the strange Saint Sammy led Gerald O'Connal to mention the Ben's new religious status. Sean was astonished, and he expressed the fear that religion was becoming like a plague you could catch. Laughingly, Mrs. O'Connal assured him that he would stop the plague before it could overcome him.

That night, as he drifted off to sleep, Brian thought over the day's events and his uncle's conversation. He also thought again of the spirea leaf, and the feeling of enchantment returned to him once more.

Downstairs, alone, Mr. and Mrs. O'Connal chatted by the fire. Maggie O'Connal reminded her husband that he had fallen asleep in church. She said that he fell asleep often lately, but, even as she spoke to him, Gerald fell asleep. She suddenly felt very afraid.

Commentary
The chapter introduces minor characters who are to be involved in episodes in later chapters: Ab, Annie and Saint Sammy (see chapters 24 to 26). The minor characters are, of course, an integral part of small-town life. Their eccentricities seem even larger than they would be among the pressing crowds of the city. Their presence adds to the vital sense of humanity that fills the small town.

Chapter 13 also introduces an element of suspense and

foreshadowing. Gerald O'Connal's habit of falling asleep frequently causes his wife anxiety. They are not an old couple—Mrs. O'Connal is only 40—but doubts about the future are raised.

CHAPTER 14

Summary

Jappy, Brian's dog, was not a model pet. He was, in fact, undisciplined and rather wild. However, he had one great virtue in Brian's eyes: he was swift and sure in hunting gophers.

One day, Forbsie Hoffman, now nicknamed "Fat," Art Sherry, Brian and Bobbie decided to go out on the prairie to hunt gophers. Their activity was essentially a rather cruel game. Brian's and Forbsie's dogs found a gopher's hole. Then the boys flooded the hole with water. When the frantic gopher emerged, it was tormented by the boys and their dogs. On this day, they were successful. Jappy chased and injured a gopher. Then Art swung the gopher in the air to snap off its tail. When the tail broke off, the gopher flew through the air and landed with a thud, pursued by the dogs. At that moment, though, the Young Ben appeared and intervened. He swiftly grabbed the wounded creature and mercifully put it to death. He then turned upon Art and gave him a merciless beating before running off home to Haggerty's Coulee.

Brian watched the proceedings with fascination. As he stared at the Young Ben, he was overcome once more with that feeling he had known when gazing at the spirea leaf. It was a feeling he had experienced on many occasions that summer. Now he knew that the Young Ben was, somehow, linked with that feeling. Brian felt confident then that what the Young Ben had done was right and proper, and he wished that he could have done it.

Brian thought about that incident often. He often went out to Haggerty's Coulee in the hope of meeting the Young Ben, but he was not successful.

On one occasion, he took Bobbie with him, and they found the remains of the tailless gopher on an ant hill. Bobbie began to cry at the sight of the ugliness of the decaying animal. The effect upon Brian was very different and very dramatic. That old, familiar feeling came back to him, now stronger and wilder. He experienced a sudden insight into the terror of the prairie, which seemed to be governed by a vast, menacing spirit, indifferent to the lives of its creatures.

The Ben's membership in the church lasted only three weeks. His welcome ended when the still he had in the basement exploded and filled the church with the smell of fermenting liquor. The Ben worked feverishly during the service to remove traces of his still. Consequently, there was not enough evidence to prosecute him for the illegal still, but Mr. Powelly swore to have his revenge.

Commentary

In a preface to the novel, W.O. Mitchell declared:

In this story I have tried to present sympathetically the struggle of a boy to understand what still defeats mature and learned men—the ultimate meaning of the cycle of life. To him are revealed in moments of fleeting vision the realities of birth, hunger, satiety, eternity, death.

Chapter 14 presents the reader with one of those "moments." In the incident with the gopher, Brian is aware of the sanctity of life. Thus, he is repelled by Art's cruelty toward the living creatures of the prairie. For that reason, he admires the Young Ben's intervention. As a result, he experiences feelings like those he knew when gazing at the spirea leaf. The intervention was a moment of magic, filled with a sense of rightness and justice. Beauty had been defiled, and revenge had been exacted. However, at this point, Brian's vision needs to be extended. Nature is not all poetry; life is not all magic. Thus, the feelings aroused by the sight of the decaying gopher provide a necessary part of the vision. He needs to understand also the essential grimness of existence; he needs to hear not just the song of joy, but also the song of lamentation.

CHAPTER 15

Summary

The fall brought a new teacher, Miss Thompson, to replace Miss MacDonald. As Mr. Digby spoke with her just before registration time, he judged that she was a determined young woman, perhaps 26 or 27, with an attractive, girlish quality.

He discovered that she had taught for five years in Azure, where Peter Svarich had had his practice. She had known Svarich then, but she was not about to volunteer any more information. As they talked, Mr. Digby began to become rather attracted to her, and regretted the frayed sleeves of his shirt.

Mr. Digby showed her about the town and then left her to make her way home. She was living in a cottage on the other side of the railway tracks with Miss Taylor from the telephone office and Miss James of Blaine's store. As she crossed the bridge over the river and saw the tar-paper shacks of German Town, she concluded that her home was definitely on the wrong side of town. She stopped for a moment to recall the past. She had noticed Peter Svarich's office and remembered his parents. His mother had been a hard-working peasant woman. His father had been a small, impish-looking man with twinkling eyes. She knew now what she had not realized then: Peter had been ashamed of his foreign origins.

Mr. Digby was usually careless about his dress. Having met Miss Thompson, he now decided that he should have his only pair of shoes repaired. He went to Wilt Palmer's Shoe and Harness Shop. When he visited Mr. Palmer, Mr. Digby would usually take an armload of books and depart with a similar armload. Mr. Palmer was something of a philosopher. However, when he had settled down with a glass of the Ben's brew, Mr. Palmer surprised him by stating that the books did not matter. He had, he explained, decided to give up thinking. Rather than being a man, he wished that he could be a tree. A tree survived without thinking. In the conversation, it emerged that Mr. Palmer's new attitude probably had been caused by a dispute with Mr. Powelly. The minister had come to the shop trying to find out where the Ben had hidden his still. The two had had a long talk about God, and Mr. Palmer declared that God and Mr. Powelly had not fared very well in the dispute.

The conversation was interrupted by the arrival of Bobbie O'Connal, who wanted to know whether the harnessmaker was making anything today that he could watch. Mr. Palmer told him that only Mr. Digby's shoes were being repaired; he should come back the next day.

Mr. Palmer continued to explain his new thoughts. There were two kinds of reality, he suggested: the real, and what a man figures to be real. The real, he insisted, is composed of birth and death and whatever lies between the two. Mr. Digby suggested that he needed to read Ecclesiastes.

Brian entered, looking for Bobbie. As he left, he noticed that Mr. Digby had a hole in his sock.

Commentary

This chapter offers the most extensive portrait so far of Milt Palmer. He is a hard-working, thoughtful man, with an attractive, human quality. He is antagonistic toward Mr. Powelly, because he sees the essential hardness of the minister. The philosophy that the harnessmaker explains to Mr. Digby is the philosophy of the honest, working man who is close to life's tribulations and to man's troubles. It is interesting to note that, in Chapter 31, Brian shares his experience of his special "feeling" in a conversation with Milt Palmer.

The chapter mentions briefly the continuing feud between the Ben and the minister. Mr. Powelly is still determined to have his revenge, with which he has some success in Chapter 16.

The most important element of plot that arises in this chapter is the arrival of Miss Thompson. On the one hand, there is an element of mystery in her previous association with Dr. Svarich. That subplot is pursued in later chapters. On the other hand, there is Mr. Digby's enchantment with the young woman, an attraction that is no less warm because he is 12 years older than she is.

CHAPTER 16

Summary

Miss Thompson was a welcome change from Miss MacDonald, but she was not weak. For example, when Fat misbehaved, he was taken out and spanked. This punishment was far more humiliating that being strapped on the hands.

There was also more freedom in the classroom. The only favoritism Miss Thompson showed was toward the "China Kids," Tang and Vooie. She had good reason for favoring them. Tang was usually ostracized by the other girls, who followed Mariel Abercrombie's leadership. Vooie was influenced by his father's fatalistic attitude.

Mr. Wong was a problem. After the death of his wife, he had retreated to his kitchen, resentful of the world. The Bluebird Cafe became dirty and neglected. Finally, toward the end of October, Miss Thompson, worried about the lack of energy displayed by the Wong children, consulted Dr. Svarich. At first, he was hostile. His relationship with Miss Thompson had been intimate, and her appearance in his office seemed to anger and upset him. However, when he saw that she was genuinely concerned about the children, Dr. Svarich softened his attitude. The children, he explained, were suffering from malnutrition. He advised her to talk to Mr. Wong. As she left the office, Ruth Thompson reflected on Peter Svarich's personality. Everyone's first impression of him was mistaken, she thought. His outer defence of irony gave the impression that he was selfish and superficial. She knew that was not a true impression. He was bitter and unyielding, but not shallow. Consequently, when she had ended their relationship, the moment had been unpleasant.

When Miss Thompson saw Mr. Wong, she discovered that he had been feeding the children oatmeal mush three times a day. He had enough oatmeal left for only one more day. Filled with determination, the teacher went to see the town mayor, Mr. Neally. He was busy shaving a customer and was not interested in solving the problems of the Wong family. The matter, he explained, was under consideration. It would take time. There were problems: there were a lot of people needing relief, and the Wongs, being Chinese, were different. Miss Thompson stormed out of the shop. When she had left, Mr. Neally remarked sarcastically to his customer, Judge Mortimer, that the newcomer was trying to run the town already.

That evening, Miss Thompson visited Mr. Digby and explained the plight of the Wong children. He agreed to split the cost of the Wongs' grocery bill with her. After she had left, Digby's room felt emptier. Miss Thompson was an impressive young woman. She had, for example, rolled her own cigarette and had informed him that she could drive a binder and break a horse.

At the end of the month, Miss Thompson and Mr. Digby discovered that Peter Svarich had paid the Wongs' grocery bill.

The Young Ben was also the object of Miss Thompson's concern. Drawn sympathetically by his personality, she understood that school was a place where he felt trapped and caught. So, she ignored his truancy, with Mr. Digby's consent. She also gave the Young Ben jobs to do and errands to run.

Digby changed. In November, he bought himself a new suit. However, his efforts to spruce up his appearance to impress Miss Thompson were not totally successful.

The Ben had not changed. He had found a new hiding-place for his still: it was under three feet of manure in the cow barn. In spite of Mr. Powelly's unceasing quest for revenge, the Ben even expanded his business of selling illicit liquor. His regular customers included Joe Pivott, Sean O'Connal, Peter Svarich and Milt Palmer. Mr. Powelly gained some satisfaction the following spring when Milt Palmer was fined $25 and costs by Judge Mortimer for having some of the Ben's brew. Soon after, the judge became a customer.

Commentary

The social criticism in this chapter is worthy of note. The town has problems. Poor crop years have led to unemployment and poverty. There are people being paid relief, so that the situation of the Wong children is not unique. Nevertheless, the attitude of the mayor, Mr. Neally, to those problems is startling. Obviously, he does not wish to take swift action. Relief is an unwelcome necessity that is given grudgingly. In addition, his unyielding prejudice makes him even more unwilling to help the Wongs. They are Chinese, and, he concludes, they should be taken care of by their own kind. Unfortunately, he is not alone in his prejudice. At school, for example, Tang finds herself excluded from childhood games with the other girls, who follow the lead of the snobbish Mariel Abercrombie. Thus, the small town is by no means idyllic, and the novel is not simply a pastoral romance. The harshness of reality is readily apparent.

In this chapter, Ruth Thompson emerges as a major figure. The contrast with Miss MacDonald is striking. Miss MacDonald was harsh in her discipline; Ruth is firm and understanding. Miss MacDonald was sadistic; Ruth is compassionate. Miss MacDonald was paranoid and insecure; Ruth is self-confident and decisive. In addition, Ruth Thompson reveals clearly her intelligence and shrewdness. She concludes quickly that the town will give no help to the Wongs, and she enlists the help of the people whom she knows can be trusted to act—Mr. Digby and Peter Svarich. Evidently, she is a young woman who understands other people, as we see also in her summing up of Peter Svarich's personality. Yet, at the same time, she is hardly conventional. She rolls and smokes her own cigarettes and, as she reveals, can drive a binder and break a horse.

CHAPTER 17

Summary

As Christmas approached, Brian asked for skates. Mrs. O'Connal could hardly believe his request. She reminded him that he was only seven and that Forbsie did not have skates yet, but he retorted that Art, who was only 18 months older, did have skates. The skates became the most frequent topic of conversation in the house during the month of December.

When new tube skates appeared in the window of the hardware store, Brian asked his father if he could have them, perhaps for Christmas. He was told again that he was not old enough, but Mr. O'Connal persuaded his wife that perhaps their son should have skates as a gift. Brian was told of the possibility. Consequently, the days before Christmas were filled with excited anticipation.

On Christmas morning, Brian tore open the one parcel he had been waiting for. To his bitter disappointment, he found a pair of bob skates—skates with double runners. Finally, his disappointment causing him to lapse into silence, he left the house to try out the skates. He discovered that he could not make them work at all. He could slide and slip, but he could not skate. He sat on the ice and cried.

When Brian returned home, Uncle Sean diagnosed the problem. He explained that bob skates were no good for skating, only for being pulled. Mrs. O'Connal was so troubled by her son's disappointment that she got Mr. Harris to open his store so she could buy the tube skates.

That night, when Mrs. O'Connal checked on the children, she found Brian fast asleep, with one hand clenching the runner of one skate.

Commentary

The chapter tells of one small step in the unfolding of Brian's growing-up. He is, of course, still a child. His persistence in asking for the skates is ample illustration of that fact. In addition, the romantic dream he builds up around the skates shows his childlike imagination. His skates will be more impressive than those of Art, who only has cut-down girls' skates. Thus, when reality—in the shape of the bob skates—pushes its way into his life, he is not able to find a way to manage it. He is overcome by his bitter disappointment. Nonetheless, his life is moving on. The early chapters showed him very much as a child, with his life circumscribed by his family and by his explorations of the small town. Attending school was the first major widening of his horizons. In this chapter, he is seen emerging from childhood into boyhood.

Once again, Mrs. O'Connal's tenderness is seen in the novel. In the first few chapters, she was a mother whose life and personality were dominated by her younger son's illness. As a result, Brian felt excluded from the warmth of his mother's love and attention. The true, caring Mrs. O'Connal was witnessed in her interview with Miss MacDonald, when she reminded Miss MacDonald of the love that seemed to be absent in the teacher's life and work.

In this chapter, her caring is evident in her decisive solution to Brian's disappointment. She realizes her mistake swiftly; the bob skates were not a practical answer to Brian's request. She remedies that fault without hesitation.

CHAPTER 18

Summary

At school, the big news for the boys was Fat Hoffman's rabbits. He had two, one of them a gray Belgium. At recess, Brian and Art arranged to go home with him at four in order to help build a pen for them.

At recess, Miss Thompson kept Mariel Abercrombie in the classroom. She wanted to talk to the girl about a troublesome matter. Today was Tang's birthday, and all the girls were invited to the Wongs' house for a party after school. The teacher had overheard the girls talking before school, and it seemed that no one would be going to the party. She reminded Mariel of the party and asked her if she was going to attend. The girl was defiant. She would not be going, she announced, because her mother had told her not to go.

For the rest of the school day, Miss Thompson's mind was on the problem. After school, she sat thoughtfully in the classroom, smoking a cigarette. The women of the town, she reflected, were good women. Perhaps at today's parent-teachers meeting, she could talk to Mrs. Abercrombie. She decided sadly that that would accomplish nothing. As she sat watching a single crow in the sky outside, she recalled an old saying: "One crow, sorrow—two crows, joy."

Miss Thompson left the school to go downtown. As she walked, she passed the Hoffmans' yard, where Fat, Brian, Art and Bobbie were struggling to make a pen for the rabbits. On the way to O'Connal's drug store, a variety of people acknowledged her: adults, children, and even the Ben. She greeted them all with the same quiet friendliness. She bought a small bottle of cheap perfume and a birthday card from Mr. O'Connal.

Old Wong had the food ready for the party. The children were upstairs. Tang and Vooie were sitting silently. Tang whispered her thanks for Miss Thompson's gifts. The young girl knew that her schoolmates would not come to the house. As Miss Thompson left, Mr. Wong, busy with sandwiches and cocoa, still had not realized that there would not be any guests.

Upset, Miss Thompson made her way to the parent-teachers meeting. She was stopped momentarily by Peter

Svarich, who had noticed her troubled face. When she told him what had happened, he explained that she could not expect anything else. She was not important enough to have influence in the town. What she should do, he continued, was to marry an important man, such as himself. Then she could go to work at changing things. She did not treat his proposal seriously; he had mentioned it lightly, because that was his way of protecting himself. But she knew that he was hurt.

She was late for the meeting, but they had not waited for her. Mrs. Bowdage had already given her talk on democracy when Miss Thompson arrived.

Commentary

The most important element in the chapter is, once again, the social criticism. The spitefulness of the children and their mothers is clearly demonstrated. The Wongs, it is obvious, are socially unacceptable. Previously, no one was willing to help them in their distress. Now, the Wong children are treated as outcasts. The ringleader in this cruel campaign is obviously Mrs. Abercrombie, a woman whose stubborn narrow-mindedness had already resulted in the departure of her previous minister, Mr. Hislop. Her daughter, Mariel, has the same personality as her mother. Snobbish and nasty, she makes a game of ridiculing and hurting the Wong children. All of this behavior shows the bigotry and cruelty in the town. There is, of course, a superficial appearance of neighborliness. The men have their friendly conversations in the stores; the women take part in the activities that lead to good works; the children enjoy their innocent games. However, it is not an innocent town in which Brian grows up. Money and influence are important. The poor and humble are often the victims of those who have power.

The chapter introduces Fat's rabbits into the plot. In the next chapter, they are to bring Brian face to face again with the mystery of birth.

CHAPTER 19

Summary

The number of Fat's rabbits swelled to 10, the Belgian hare having proved to be a fruitful mother. The boys reacted to this event with wonderment and delight. Fat declared that, as the rabbits multiplied, they would be able to sell them. Brian approached his father for an explanation of the mystery of birth. With difficulty, Gerald O'Connal reminded Brian of the pigeons, which had been born from eggs that the mother carried. The seed, he explained, was planted by the father. Brian then realized that, when he had watched the rabbits, he had seen the seeds being planted in the mother. The conversation ended when Bobbie, to Brian's disgust, asked if the male rabbit could plant turnip seeds in the mother.

Fat's rabbits multiplied all summer, until there were 123 in all. The boys had increasing difficulty in finding food for them and in building enough pens to house them. Much to Fat's dismay, Mr. Hoffman announced that they would have to get rid of the rabbits. Though a tender-hearted man, he was determined to rid himself of the problem. First he made a trip to O'Connal's drugstore, and then, with the help of Joe Pivott and Mr. O'Connal, he loaded the squealing rabbits into sacks. They were taken and dumped in the river behind the *Times* building.

Brian was shocked at the killing of the rabbits, although he was not emotionally upset, as Fat was. Rather, he felt uneasiness, because the action reminded him of Art's treatment of the gopher a year earlier. What he now called "the feeling" was important to him, and he wanted to discover its meaning. So important was it to him that he had not shared his secret with anyone.

Mr. O'Connal's explanation of the mystery of birth had not entirely satisfied Brian. Consequently, he went to talk to his grandmother, whose rheumatism now often confined her to a room on the second floor. She told him impatiently that he seemed to know the how of birth and conception, whereas the why was another thing altogether. That, she declared, was God's doing. That information seemed to astonish Brian, who answered, "God isn't very considerate—is He, Gramma?"

Commentary

The picture of Fat Hoffman's rabbits is one of the truly hilarious scenes in the novel. The notion of the rabbits' prodigious fruitfulness, far outstripping the boys' efforts to feed and house them, is a comic delight. Added to that is Mr. Hoffman's frantic endeavor to segregate the sexes, an endeavor that is a total failure. The result is a virtual sea of rabbits of all shapes and sizes, engaged in a bewildering variety of activities, all of them driving Mr. Hoffman to distraction.

In this chapter, Brian takes one more step on the road to maturity. He has now seen a mammal give live birth. As a result, he comes to an understanding of the mysteries of conception and birth. However, it is Grandmother MacMurray who supplies a necessary ingredient in Brian's sex education: the spiritual element that takes sex out of the realm of mere information.

CHAPTER 20

Summary

The crop was a failure again in the fall. As a result, more families moved out, abandoning their homes and farms. More of the unemployed rode the freight trains. In town, houses were neglected, the cars were older and businesses were closed. But Sean O'Connal was almost happy. His irrigation project had worked. Now he was trying to interest farmers in damming the river in order to irrigate larger areas.

That fall, Brian's grandmother fell ill with a bad cold. That fall also, the problem of the Wongs was solved. Digby, Miss Thompson and Peter Svarich got the town to put the family on relief until the children could be sent away. Two weeks after Tang had gone to an uncle in Vancouver and Vooie to a home in Winnipeg, Mr. Wong hanged himself. In spite of the gossip among the townsfolk, no opium was found among his effects.

One Saturday in September, Brian, Fat and Bobbie stood in front of the O'Connal house. They could not decide what to do to amuse themselves. When Joe Pivott appeared with his dray, they gladly accepted the opportunity for a ride. They rode with him to the grain elevator beside the railroad tracks.

The boys then decided to visit Thorborn's Livery Stable. When they got there, they were told that inside there was a calf with two heads. The calf was dead, but it had been born with two heads. The sight confused Brian. He felt that he was seeing something that he should not be seeing. This feeling was not the same as he had experienced when gazing at the spirea leaf: it was more like the uneasiness he had known when he had seen the dead gopher.

Even when the boys joined Art to go shooting marbles in the schoolyard, Brian could not forget the sight of the calf with two heads. The memory made him think that now he would never find out the meaning of "the feeling."

Early in October, he was still thinking about the calf as he walked home from school. Then, suddenly, as he turned onto Sixth Street, Jappy ran out in front of Joe Pivott's dray. One of the horses reared at the sight of the dog, and the rear wheel of the dray caught Jappy. The dog had died by the time Brian got him to the garage at the rear of the house.

Brian buried Jappy on the prairie. As he covered the dog's body with soil, he could not believe that his pet was not going to emerge suddenly to greet him. When he had finished his unpleasant task, the Young Ben appeared. Silently, he showed Brian how to cover the grave with stones, so that the coyotes would not dig for the body.

Something had changed for Brian. He now felt an emptiness he had not known before.

Commentary

Though the picture is only briefly sketched, W.O. Mitchell presents a telling portrait of Prairie problems in the drought years. The crop was crucial to Prairie communities; their economy was based on the crop. Failure brought massive dislocation as families lost their homes and businesses failed.

The tragedy of the Wong family can hardly be stressed too much. The townsfolk had failed to realize that Mr. Wong's failure as a father and as a businessman was caused by his grief over the death of his wife. They had sneeringly suggested that he was an opium addict. The depth of Mr. Wong's love for his family emerged, however, when the children were taken from him. He chose death. That death is a witness to the prejudice and indifference displayed by the influential people of the town.

The incident with the two-headed calf is a confusing moment for Brian in his exploration of the meaning of life. It is, for him, as perplexing as the feeling he had known on the prairie when he gazed at the remains of the dead gopher. The confusion of feelings is, of course, natural. Brian has yet to

45

fully understand the mystery of this world, in which the good and the bad, the beautiful and the ugly, the joyful and the sorrow-laden, co-exist.

Most important, however, is the death of Jappy. For the first time, Brian has to grapple with the loss of something dear to him, something vital, alive and responsive. He now knows the ache that death brings.

PART III • CHAPTER 21

Summary

Two years had passed since the death of Jappy. Brian, now almost 10, was nicknamed Chirp because he could make the sound of baby chicks cheeping. In school, he had come into Mr. Digby's class.

It was another drought year. The rain, coming in early July, had arrived too late. Now, in late July, the hot winds swept over the prairie.

One afternoon, Brian sat on the porch of his home. He thought lazily of going swimming, but dismissed the idea. The low river caused prairie itch, which raised small blisters. Also, the walk to the river seemed long to him at this moment.

In her room, Grandmother MacMurray sat in her rocker by the window. She was now 80, her face showed her age, and she knew that her grip on life was weak. As she rocked, she thought of homesteading days with her husband, John. She imagined herself riding in the buckboard with John, when Riel had been hanged, Quebec had turned Liberal, and Maggie had not yet been born. Her time was short, she reflected. One bad cold would take her off; the last one almost had.

On the porch below, Brian watched Joe Pivott's panting setter. An unwelcome thought came into his mind. At the bidding of the thought, he threw a pebble at the dog, but the animal ignored him. He decided to see what Fat and Art were doing.

Upstairs, Bobbie opened the window wider for his grandmother. His reward was a chocolate. As he ate it, Mrs. MacMurray told him about his dead grandfather. He had been a skilled fiddler, who could make his fiddle produce all kinds of sounds. He had fiddled, the grandmother explained, to make people laugh, and he had fiddled to make them cry. Bobbie asked her to tell him again the story of grandfather and the bobcat.

Gerald O'Connal stood in the doorway of his drugstore. He was concerned about his habit of falling asleep, which had got worse. He could feel it coming upon him even now. He decided that he must speak to Peter Svarich again.

In the Royal Hotel beer parlor, the Ben, with a 50-pound

sack of feed on his head, was regaling with stories a traveller for the MacDougall Implement Company. His reward was free beer.

In the Presbyterian manse, Mr. Powelly was choosing his text for Sunday. His theme, he decided, would be "Vital Things," and his text, "I am the vine, ye are the branches."

Brian, Art and Fat were walking out to visit Saint Sammy. Only Art had been there before. Sammy, he told his friends, was a crazy bachelor who lived alone on the prairie. As they approached Sammy's piano-box home, they encountered a terrible stench. It was "dead-cow stink," Art assured them. The smell and the thought of meeting crazy Sammy were enough for Fat. He went back home. However, as Brian and Art came closer, they, too, grew afraid: perhaps Sammy was lying dead. Then Sammy appeared, welcoming the boys. He was a wild-looking man, his face covered with whiskers. His talk was rambling and incoherent and filled with religious ravings. Bent Candy would not get his horses, he declared. God had assured him that they would be shod with silver horseshoes, and that their harness would have diamonds, emeralds and gold. As he talked, he held a battered tin box containing his treasures: underwear labels, matchboxes, bits of twig and stone, broken china, stove bolts, safety pins and pencil stubs.

His talk consisted of God's revelations to him. God, he said, had condemned the town. The droughts were God's punishment, for the people of the town had played "the harlot and the fornicator." Prompted by Art, Saint Sammy gave his own wild, poetic account of the Creation story. Then, abruptly, he dismissed the boys, declaring that the Lord was waiting for him.

On the walk home, Brian's thoughts revealed that he had been spellbound by the encounter with Saint Sammy. The old feeling had come back to the boy, even though he knew very well that Sammy was crazy. For a few moments, the boy "had been alive as he had never been before, passionate for the thing that slipped through the grasp of his understanding and eluded him."

Commentary
Significant plot elements are clearly indicated in this part of

48

the narrative. Most important is the emphasis upon Mr. O'Connal's health. It has deteriorated, and his sleepiness has become worse. In addition, Mrs. MacMurray's aging is stressed. She spends more time in her room and more time reminiscing about the past.

The most significant aspect of the chapter, though, is the meeting with Saint Sammy. He is a wild mystic, living in a piano box on the prairie, passionately attached to his fine team of horses. However, his ravings are not entirely without sense. He is a man convicted by a vision of God, whom he sees as all-powerful and all-knowing. Such is the power of his vision that Brian is enchanted. The boy makes the connection between Sammy's passion and his own "feeling." That "feeling" has been seen in various aspects in the novel so far. At first, it was only a vague response to the majesty of the prairie and the Young Ben's place in it. Later, with the gopher incident and with the vision of the spirea leaf, the feeling took on the quality of a mystical reverence for life. After the conversation between Digby and Milt Palmer, the feeling was revealed as having some connection with a quest for meaning, a quest for answers to significant questions. In this chapter, another aspect of the feeling is suggested. The feeling has to do with knowledge, with knowing about significant things, but the questions themselves are important, too—"It wouldn't be so bad, Brian thought, if a person knew, or even knew what it was that he wanted to know."

CHAPTER 22

Summary

Bobbie O'Connal saw Art and Brian walking in the road by MacTaggart's Corner. He hurried after them, but he was not welcome. The boys had built a hut on Campbell's vacant lot at the end of Sixth Street and they were going there to smoke. Bobbie insisted that he knew what they were going to do. When Art was rude to Bobbie, Brian, who was loyal to his brother, allowed Bobbie to go with them as far as Fat's.

At Fat's, the boys, who wanted to go to the hut to smoke, waited while they tried to solve the problem of Bobbie's presence. Brian was not keen on smoking, anyway. It made him hot, and Fat had been sick three times.

Art mentioned that Pinky Funder's mother had had a new baby the night before. Bobbie asked innocently how it was that the Funders had a new baby every year, because they had no gooseberry bushes. His remark drew Art's scorn. Babies, he declared were made by one's father and mother, just like other animals. Brian, trying to protect his brother's innocence, protested that it was not the same. In answer to Art's statement, he insisted that he had not come out of his mother's belly-button. God, he stated, sent babies. Brian and Bobbie left the Hoffmans' yard to the accompaniment of the jeers of the other boys. As they walked away, Brian warmed to Bobbie's naïve insistence that God sends babies. As he sent his brother home, Brian concluded that Bobbie was all right.

As Brian made his way to the hut, he saw the Young Ben. He felt the familiar attraction to the older boy, but resisted the impulse to approach him. Inside the hut, he thought bitterly of what had happened. He felt now that he would never know what he wanted to know. The feeling was no good.

The Young Ben, meanwhile, was staring in the window of Harris' Hardware, looking yearningly at a gun on display. He was approached by Mr. Digby, who had noticed the look on the boy's face. The Young Ben turned away silently. Mr. Digby knew that the Young Ben wanted the gun badly. He also wanted something badly: to marry Miss Thompson. The night before, he had reasoned out the matter carefully. He had not much to offer. His salary was small, he did not have a university degree, and being a teacher's wife did not bring much social status. But, he had concluded, though he could not offer as much as Peter Svarich, the matter was still possible. Now, he was not as sure as he had been. He was, he decided, no more likely to get Miss Thompson than the Young Ben was to get his gun.

Brian returned home, but found no one in the living room. Moreover, the cuckoo clock had not been wound. His father always did that when he came home. Then he saw Bobbie, who had been crying. He told Brian that their father was very sick; his gall bladder was malfunctioning. All afternoon, Brian worried about his father, whom he was not allowed to see. At supper, he found it difficult to be interested in food. He finally got up to see his father, but was met by his mother, who warned him to be quiet by putting a finger to her lips. The boy and his mother walked downstairs, arm in arm. As he felt the pressure of her arm around him, Brian was suddenly overcome by a strong sense of "the feeling."

Commentary

While Mr. O'Connal's illness advances the plot, the major concern of this chapter is the further revelation of Brian's special feeling. The first episode involves Brian's bitter sense of frustration in the conversation with Art. Brian knows the facts of life. He knows how babies are made. He has already made the connection between the rabbits and human beings in their reproductive activities. However, sensitive as he is, he is not willing to ignore the spiritual aspects of human reproduction. Human beings, he insists, are *not* exactly like the animals; the difference is the activity of God. In a real sense, he feels, God sends babies to humans. For that reason, Brian seeks to protect his little brother's innocence, feeling something essentially right about Bobbie's attitude. Brian is unable, though, to fight successfully against Art's declarations. The problem is too big for Brian, too full of the unknown. Hence, he gives up in frustration. However, a more significant moment occurs later in the chapter. Faced with the fact of his father's illness and embraced by his mother, Brian experiences the return of the feeling. Clearly, that feeling is of a different quality from Brian's earlier sense of reverence for the beauty of all created things. Now, the feeling is associated with the significance of death in human existence and with the reassurance of love in the scheme of things. The feeling is part of the process of asking questions and seeking answers. It is part of what W.O. Mitchell describes as "the struggle of a young boy to understand what still defeats mature and learned men—the ultimate meaning of the cycle of life and death."

CHAPTER 23

Summary

The condition of Mr. O'Connal's gall bladder was serious. He would have to go on a diet, rest for a month and then go to

Rochester for an operation. Though he objected, his wife insisted that arrangements could be made. Leon, the clerk, could look after the store, Mrs. MacMurray could look after Bobbie, and Brian could go to his Uncle Sean's. She was not, however, happy about the last part of the arrangements.

Like most of the other farmers, Sean had experienced crop failure. His successful garden was no consolation, for he had not been able to interest other farmers in his scheme to dam the river. As a last resort, he had gone to Bent Candy, the Baptist deacon, who had been lucky with his land. Mr. Candy had declared flatly that he was not interested in garden irrigation, strip farming or damming the river. The more Sean had cursed, the more adamant Candy had become. After Sean's angry departure, Mr. Candy had sat down to prepare for his prayer meeting, at which the new minister was to be taken to task for using the Moffat translation of the Bible.

Afterward, Sean gave up all hope of persuading others of the rightness of his schemes. Even his cook, Annie, was no longer a source of joy, because she doted hopelessly on Ab, the hired man, who had become more and more evangelistic. It was Ab's faith that finally convinced Mrs. O'Connal that Brian should stay with Sean.

The Ben was ill. Lying in a drunken stupor on the sidewalk, he had been visited by botflies, which hatched in his ear. The Ben's plight only increased Mr. Powelly's determination to have his revenge upon the man. That determination had been increased by the information that, when the Young Ben stole a rifle and cartridges from Harris' Hardware, Mr. Digby had paid for the articles, thus saving the boy from prosecution. Mr. Powelly decided to have a talk with Digby.

The minister's visit ended a bad day for Digby. That afternoon, he had taken Miss Thompson for tea. Then he had proposed marriage. She had been astonished at his suggestion. She was fond of him, she had admitted, but Peter Svarich was first in her affections. Later, Miss Thompson thought about Mr. Digby's proposal. It intrigued her, but she wished he had not asked. She was going to marry Peter Svarich after school ended for the year. Yet she could not feel sorry for Digby, not the way she might have for Svarich. That was the difference between the two men that inclined her to Svarich: Digby could take care of himself.

Mr. Powelly came to remonstrate with Mr. Digby for paying for the stolen gun for the Young Ben. The boy, the minister insisted, should have been sent to reform school. However, the teacher soon reduced Mr. Powelly to utter confusion. At first, Powelly stated that the Young Ben should have been prosecuted because his father was a drunken sinner. Then he protested that prosecution would be for the good of the town. Finally, he stammered that it would be for the Young Ben's own good. At that point, Digby began to question the minister about his philosophical beliefs. Mr. Powelly was flustered and prepared to leave, but Digby would not let him go. The Young Ben, he tried to explain, was different. Moreover, he had never done any harm to the town; he did not even associate with the other boys. When the minister retorted that perhaps the case should be reopened, Mr. Digby indicated that, as far as he was concerned, the matter was closed. Mr. Powelly left, observing that Digby's attitude was going to make it more difficult for him to do what he felt had to be done. Digby knew Powelly's real motive: hatred of the Ben.

Commentary

Plot elements are developed quickly in this chapter. First, the crisis presented by Gerald O'Connal's illness has emerged clearly. Not only does it mean changes in the O'Connal household, it also foreshadows future complications. In addition, the subplot involving Sean and his struggle for efficient prairie farming is carried forward. His task is seen to be formidable. The romantic subplot is also further developed. Digby's love for Miss Thompson has been expressed at last, but she seems to have decided firmly in Peter Svarich's favor. Finally, there is one more skirmish in the war between Mr. Powelly and the Ben. The minister's irrational conduct makes him a dangerous foe.

CHAPTER 24

Summary

After his parents had left for Rochester, Brian drove with

Uncle Sean out to his uncle's farm. Sean cursed all the way; he cursed the government for the roads, and he cursed the drought, the weeds, the car, the distance to the farm, the flat tire, the car brakes, the farm gate and his dog, Buck. When they arrived at the house, he simply cursed.

Brian went with Ab to feed the pigs. One of them, Brian discovered, was misshapen and unhealthy. Ab explained that it was a runt.

In the evenings, Brian was allowed to stay up until the flame flickered in the coal-oil lamp. He used to trace the pictures of horses he found in the Hudson Bay catalogue. Ab would read the *Prairie Farm Review*, searching for a cure for Noreen, their asthmatic Holstein cow. Annie would sit sewing, so that the terrible cast in her right eye could hardly be noticed. Sean sat silently smoking his pipe.

On the third evening, Sean, who never spoke directly to Ab, mentioned casually that the runt pig would have to be looked after. The next morning, Ab, followed by Brian, took a hammer and went toward the pigs. When Brian realized that taking care of the runt meant killing it, Brian objected and began swearing. Ab beat him for using such language, but Brian did not stop. His own fluency in cursing surprised him, and Ab chased him. Sean joined in the chase and gave Brian another spanking. However, at Annie's suggestion, the runt was allowed to live, on condition that Brian fed it with a bottle.

As time passed, Brian came to understand the depth of Annie's affection for Ab. She wanted very much to marry Ab. Then, two weeks later, Brian came across the solution to the problem. In the Hudson Bay catalogue, he found an advertisement for spectacles that would straighten the cast in Annie's eye. He persuaded Annie to write for spectacles. A difficulty arose though: Annie would have to go to Regina to have her eyes tested. Again, Brian solved the problem. Annie would see Dr. Svarich and complain of stomach trouble. He would order her to go to Regina for two or three days.

The plan worked perfectly. Annie returned from Regina, and her eye was now perfectly straight behind her glasses. Strangely, though, Ab's attitude to Annie in the following days was cool. One evening, Brian discovered what was the matter. Ab confessed that he had intended to marry Annie before; now he was not going to do so. Brian pondered over Ab's words. The world, he decided, was a funny place. He loved a runt pig "that wasn't good for anything," and Ab made a fuss of Noreen, the cow that coughed and sneezed. Before her eye was straightened, Ab loved Annie. In a flash, the solution came to Brian, and he hurried to tell Annie about it.

Commentary

The chapter reveals more of Brian's reverence for living things. His sense of outrage over the planned killing of the runt pig is vivid evidence of the boy's sensitivity. However, that reverence for life takes on a new dimension with the episode dealing with Annie's new spectacles. Brian becomes aware unexpectedly of the strangeness of human love. Love, he discovers, does not necessarily have anything to do with beauty or usefulness. Thus, he can love a sickly pig, and Ab can care for an asthmatic cow. Above all, Ab can love Annie, in spite of the ugly cast in her eye. Annie, in his view, does not need to be improved. He loves her for what she is. That realization is, for Brian, a moment of epiphany, a moment of insight. He has, obviously, made an important discovery about love.

The plot has taken one significant step forward. Mr. and Mrs. O'Connal have gone to Rochester, where Gerald O'Connal is to have a gall bladder operation.

CHAPTER 25

Summary

The fall was quiet. Ab was working in the blacksmith shop. Annie sang in the kitchen, looking forward to her marriage to Ab after the harvest. Brian was bored. He stared at Duke and Empress, the horses standing hitched to the half-filled manure rack. With excitement, he decided to mount the rack and drive the horses around the yard. Unfortunately for Brian, the horses were high-spirited. He lost the reins as the animals lunged forward. The cart was smashed against the gatepost, and Brian was thrown to the ground. He was unhurt, but the horses and the broken rack sped off toward the prairie. It took Ab half an hour to bring them back, and when he arrived, he was furious with Brian.

Brian, full of self-pity, concluded that Annie and Ab did not care for him at all. He decided to go back home and began to walk. As he made his way to town, he thought longingly of his grandmother and Bobbie. But, as the hours wore on, his sense of loneliness affected him strangely. He felt separate and apart from everything. He was aware of the two voices of the night wind: its humming in the wires overhead, and its deep roaring over the prairie. That night, he slept in a haystack. As he looked at the night sky, a frightening sense of his own fragility came over him.

When he awoke the next morning, he was beset by hunger and thirst. Yet, at the same time, a familiar feeling returned to him, "an experience of apartness" that was like singing. As he resumed his journey, he was overtaken by Ab. The hired man had terrible news: Brian's father had died.

Commentary

Again, there is emphasis upon two aspects of Brian's personality. On the one hand, he is a typical young boy, bored by inactivity and thinking of ways to fill time. Thus, his act of driving the horses is thoughtless and selfish. The episode could, of course, have ended tragically, for Brian or for the horses. As it was, the only damage was to the rack, which was, however, needed for the harvest. On the other hand, Brian's decision to walk back to town provides the situation in which Brian's special feeling appears again. Alone on the prairie, he experiences a unique sensation of his own being, a feeling of his own separateness and the distinct separateness of being that is the quality of all created things. His experience is mystical, like that of the poet Theordore Roethke, in "A Field of Light":

I could watch! I could watch!
I saw the separateness of all things!
My heart lifted up with the great grasses;
The weeds believed me, and the nesting birds.
There were clouds making a rout of shapes
        crosssing a windbreak of cedars,
And a bee shaking drops from a rain-soaked
        honeysuckle.
The worms were delighted as wrens.

And I walked, I walked through the light air;
I moved with the morning.

From the point of view of plot, the most important event of the chapter is the reported death of Gerald O'Connal. Brian had previously had to grapple with the death of his beloved Jappy. Now, his loving, caring father, a family man through and through, has gone. This experience provides Brian with the first critical event of his life.

CHAPTER 26

Summary

The O'Connal home was filled with funeral flowers, and all the blinds were drawn. The casket stood in the dining room. The voices of Mrs. O'Connal and the visitors seemed, to Brian, to be muffled. His mother had not cried; her voice was toneless and she seemed dazed. Brian had not cried either. He was not happy, but he did not feel like crying.

The visitors had cried. Mrs. Abercrombie had said that Mr. O'Connal was a fine man. Others had said it was a shame, that it was hard to realize that Mr. O'Connal was dead. When he looked at his grandmother, Brian felt a little like crying.

Brian went to the hut with Fat. They played cards, but Brian was not really interested. He confessed to Fat that he had not yet cried. Fat assured him that he would cry at the funeral.

In the hardware store, Mr. Harris told Mr. Digby that Mr. Powelly had called. The minister wanted to know if anything else was missing after the Young Ben had broken into the store. Mr. Harris had promised that he would check. Mr. Digby insisted that he should be informed if anything else were missing, and he would pay for the articles.

Mrs. MacMurray sat alone, thinking. Her daughter, she knew, was a good woman . . . if only she could find release in tears. Her son-in-law had been a fine man, she reflected.

Mrs. Abercrombie was asking her husband about Mr. O'Connal's estate. There, he said, $20,000, payable monthly, as well as the business.

As he lay with Bobbie asleep beside him, Brian could not get over the fact that nothing seemed to have changed. He thought again of his mother, who had not cried yet. He decided to go to his mother's room. Maggie O'Connal lay with closed eyes. Brian kissed her cheek, which was still dry. Suddenly, her eyes opened and stared at him. He went back to his room quickly, for he realized with a start that she had not even seen him.

Mr. Powelly conducted the funeral at the house. The family did not go out to the cemetery. Brian was very sad, and began to walk out to the prairie.

In her room, Mrs. MacMurray took out her worn Bible, which she had been given on her wedding in September, 1874.

On the prairie, Brian experienced a sense of the timelessness of the prairie, in contrast with the brevity of human life. People, he realized, were born and died, but the prairie was forever. Seasons came and went, but man never returned. His father would never return. His mother would be forever lonely; the silence of death would never end. The thought of his mother made Brian realize that she needed him now. He was filled with tenderness and the tears began to course down his cheeks. As a meadow lark's song rang out, a "fierce excitement" filled him. He went home to his mother.

Commentary

Mitchell shrewdly captures the atmosphere that surrounds a death in the family: the cloying perfume of the flowers, the dimness of the drawn shades, the muted conversations of the mourners. No less convincing is the portrayal of the grief of the family. Deep sorrow does not necessarily bring immediate tears. The sense of loss and the brutality of the shock at first inhibit the tears of Brian and his mother.

The chapter also presents one more step for Brian on the road to maturity. After his mystical experience on the prairie, he is better able to deal with his grief. He comes to know, with vivid insight, the brevity of man's existence. His father has gone, but the world moves on. The process, he sees, is inexorable. Thus, Brian turns to the living, to his mother. They are one in their loss. She needs him; he yearns for her.

At the same time, the world moves on in a much more cynical sense. Everyone acknowledges that Mr. O'Connal was a fine man, but the townsfolk do not change. Mrs. Abercrombie, for example, sang a hymn at the funeral, but, in her conversation with her husband, her main interest is in finding out Mrs. O'Connal's financial position. Further, Mr. Powelly has not given up his quest for revenge against the Ben and his son. He still seeks to have the Young Ben prosecuted. These petty concerns obviously offer a sharp contrast to the timeless majesty of nature.

PART IV • CHAPTER 27

Summary

Brian was surprised that, some months later, he did not think of his father for a week at a time. He did dream of him often, awaking with a sense of yearning.

His relationship with his mother became closer. He also looked after his brother more: he taught Bobbie to skate and to swim and insisted on his being allowed to play ball with the other boys. In addition, though he was only 11, Brian seemed to be closer to his grandmother, whose health had failed noticeably. She had cataracts and spent all day in her room.

Every Sunday in the spring and summer, Uncle Sean would drive the family to visit the grave, which was on the prairie about a mile from town. At such times, Brian would wonder what had happened to the special feeling he had experienced when the meadow lark had sung to him.

In the two years since his father's death, he had seldom thought of that feeling he had known so long. Bits and pieces came back to him: the dead pigeon, the gopher, the dewdrop and the two-headed calf. Then, in the spring of 1937, trying to recapture the feeling, he went out to see Saint Sammy. However, Sammy's evangelistic rantings did nothing for Brian. Perhaps he was now simply busier than he had been. He was captain of the school ball team and had played in the hockey league.

The Young Ben's interest in him did not change. The two were even closer. They walked together over the prairie or when the Young Ben delivered the washing his mother did. That winter, they ran a trapline together. Brian was the only child in the school who had conversation with the Young Ben.

Mrs. Abercrombie was now on the school board. Because of her, Digby could no longer ignore the Young Ben's truancy. She began to criticize Digby for his lack of discipline, lamenting Miss MacDonald's departure. Powelly was an enthusiastic ally. He mentioned what he regarded as Digby's unsatisfactory handling of the incident with the Young Ben the year before. The principal, he observed, did not attend church, spent time with Milt Palmer and could often be seen talking to the Ben. He suggested that Jake Harris be appointed school probation officer. Mrs. Abercrombie was grateful. Mariel, she considered, was not doing as well in school as she should be, and Mr. Digby had described the girl as lazy.

The winter had been terrible for Digby. His feelings for Miss Thompson divided him. On the one hand, he was intoxicated by her presence. On the other hand, he wished she were not there. By spring, he knew that he had become unusually irritable and visited Milt Palmer, to talk philosophy and get drunk on the Ben's brew.

That spring, a special town by-law was passed, specifically aimed at the Ben, to forbid urinating on First Street. The Ben's still was undetected.

That spring also, Brian first saw the owl that the Ben had trapped. It was caged in a chicken-netting coop in one corner of the fence. He was transfixed by the sight of the wild creature confined so pathetically, and his own being responded sympathetically to its plight. As he watched the bird, he was joined by Mr. Digby. The teacher felt the same emotions as Brian did, but there was something more. The trapped bird reminded Mr. Digby of the Young Ben in school. When Brian had left, the teacher found the Ben drunk and Mrs. Ben disinterested in discussing the Young Ben's truancy.

Mr. Digby recalled the plight of the owl for a long time afterward. It stopped bothering him when he heard that the marriage of Miss Thompson and Peter Svarich had been postponed until the fall.

The engagement of Miss Thompson and Dr. Svarich had its problems. With the success of his proposal, Svarich had, in Miss Thompson's judgment, become too self-assertive and possessive. She thought of his pride in his car and his pride in the new medical building he had built, and concluded that he had too great a need for respect and attention. Miss Thompson wrestled with the problem all spring. In her doubts, she saw more and more of Digby. Finally, she told him that the wedding was being postponed because Svarich was going away for the summer to take a refresher course.

That summer, Mr. Powelly had his revenge. While Jake Harris was visiting, the Ben's mare, Dolly, accidentally uncovered the still. At the trial, the Ben pleaded not guilty, but changed his plea when the still was offered in evidence. Judge

Mortimer pondered the case with difficulty. He flipped through a mail-order catalogue that he had brought to the courtroom instead of the Criminal Code. Finally, he sentenced the Ben to a fine of $90. Under prompting, he added the alternative of 90 days in jail.

In church that Sunday, Mr. Powelly celebrated his victory by preaching a sermon about God's vengeance. As he listened, Brian felt confused. The notion of God's wrathful punishment frightened him, but, at the same time, he considered the punishment unjust.

The Ben went to jail, for Mrs. Ben would not raise the money for the fine. Under the threat of punishment from his father, the Young Ben looked after both the Ben and the owl. Though he was probably more comfortable than he had been at any time in his life, imprisonment was hard on the Ben. At first he stormed and raged. Later, he paced his cell like a trapped animal. After watching the Ben through the cell window, Brian decided to pay a visit to Saint Sammy.

Commentary

After his bitter conversation with Mr. Powelly, in Chapter 23, Mr. Digby had noticed particularly a book among his collection. The book was *Heart of Darkness*, by Joseph Conrad, which tells the story of a good man, named Kurtz, who was led astray by the forces of evil in the human heart. Though he had good intentions in the beginning, Kurtz became a murderer and a robber. Mr. Digby has clearly realized the significance of Mr. Powelly's hatred of the Ben. It is a perverted hatred, a hatred that has overcome the minister's religious belief and Christian compassion. This chapter shows the triumph of the power of those forces. Even the town judge buys the Ben's liquor, but that does not halt the ferocity of the revenge. However, the evil forces have not stopped their work. Mrs. Abercrombie, abetted by Mr. Powelly, is beginning to move against Mr. Digby. His "crime," in their eyes, is his compassionate treatment of the Young Ben. Mrs. Abercrombie, now a member of the school board, is about to seek Mr. Digby's dismissal. It is a foreshadowing of the plot that obviously pits the evil forces and the good forces squarely against one another.

The romantic subplot is furthered in this chapter. The

engagement of Miss Thompson and Dr. Svarich does not go smoothly. The problems that plagued their relationship in earlier years reappear. Mr. Digby's chances of success seem good.

In Brian's spiritual growth, the chapter is a time of waiting. His grief over his father's death is gradually healing, but he does not experience a return of his special feeling. However, his feeling of empathy with the caged owl and his sensitivity to the plight of the jailed Ben indicate some promise of a further spiritual step.

CHAPTER 28

Summary

Saint Sammy, Jehovah's hired man, had waited for God's judgment on Bent Candy. Now, the fifth day after Candy's last visit to him, Saint Sammy knew that the day had come.

Bent Candy had added a further five sections to his land that year. He had also planted all of his land with flax. As usual, with his incredible luck he had prospered. He was now called "the Flax King."

Since Candy had first made his bid to buy the Clydesdale horses, Sammy had been reminded constantly in a vision of that fateful day 10 years ago. At that time, Sammy's crop had been ruined by hail. The Lord had bidden Sammy to take his horses to Magnus Petersen, who would allow Sammy land to live on. However, the Lord added a condition: Sammy was never to sell the horses. Then at the right time, God would take him up to heaven.

Five days ago, Bent Candy had come to Saint Sammy. He wanted the horses. When he refused, Candy told him that he had a week to get off the land; Magnus Petersen had sold out to Candy. Sammy had protested and had threatened Candy with the vengeance of the Lord. Bent Candy had remained adamant. That same evening, Sammy had gone to Bent Candy. He found Candy outside his new barn, an impressive structure built especially for the Clydesdales. Candy had no use for the animals, he farmed by tractor. But he coveted the horses. Sammy had again forewarned the farmer of God's wrath. Candy had been tormented by doubt. He dearly wanted the horses. Perhaps, he had thought, it would be better to buy new pews for the Baptist Church.

Now, on the fifth day, Sammy awaited the vengeance of the Lord. A rising wind began to stir the prairie grasses.

As he walked over the prairie, Brian began to regret his decision to visit Saint Sammy. A fierce windstorm was threatening. When he arrived, he found Sammy in the midst of the wind, rejoicing in the signs of God's vengeance against Bent Candy. The storm became fierce, and Sammy and Brian sought shelter in the piano box.

The wind blew through the town. For the first time in his jail term, the Ben stood still in the middle of his cell, listening to the storm.

Maggie O'Connal hurriedly shut her mother's bedroom window and anxiously tended to the old lady.

Mrs. Abercrombie and Mr. Powelly, planning the Ladies' Auxiliary garden party, feeling the house shake under the blast of the storm, flung themselves to their knees in prayer.

After the storm, Sammy and Brian walked over to Bent Candy's. They found the farmer standing beside the ruins of what had been his splendid new barn. Even Saint Sammy was awe-struck as he reminded Candy of what the Lord had promised. Candy said simply that Sammy could stay on the land, and added a simple "amen" to Sammy's religious outpourings.

Commentary

This chapter represents the climax of the Saint Sammy subplot. That climax comes to the reader with a mixture of amusement and wonderment. Saint Sammy is vindicated, and Bent Candy's fear is comic in its dimensions. He is literally speechless in the midst of the devastation that has come to him, and he clearly has a new respect for Sammy.

In another aspect, the chapter witnesses a victory of good over evil. Sammy is a harmless crackpot, while Bent Candy is a greedy hypocrite. He has coveted the Clydesdales against the more righteous dictates of his religious beliefs, and his wrongdoing is punished. Neither character is really a very credible human being; both portraits are caricatures. Thus, the episode appears as a kind of morality play, in which, inevitably, the good are rewarded and the evil are punished.

CHAPTER 29

Summary

The storm had damaged the town considerably—Mr. Abercrombie estimated the cost at $50,000.

Though Mrs. O'Connal worried about her mother, who had sat by the open window for several minutes during the storm, the old lady seemed to be revitalized by the event and actually came downstairs for some meals. Uncle Sean seemed similarly exuberant because none of his buildings had been damaged.

Since his brother's death, Uncle Sean seemed calmer. Ab had stopped trying to convert him and was devoting his time to his wife and family. In July, 1937, Annie gave birth to twin daughters. Uncle Sean was, however, still pessimistic about the crop.

Brian's excitement over the Sammy incident lasted for several days. The Young Ben, more restless than usual, took a week off school.

When he returned, an incident took place regarding sharpening pencils, three days before the Ben's release from jail. Mr. Digby's rule was that, while he was teaching, no pencils were to be sharpened in the part of the room where he was not teaching. The Young Ben absent-mindedly broke the rule. After school, Mr. Digby informed the Young Ben that he was now expelled. Accompanied by Brian, the boy went to the jail and informed his father that he was dropping school. The Ben's only reply was an order to let the owl go free.

Commentary

The central incident—Mr. Digby's expulsion of the Young Ben—acts as the prelude for the dramatic events of the next chapter. The principal has struggled for years with the problem of the Young Ben. He has responded sympathetically to the boy's yearning for freedom; he has tried to enlist the aid of the boy's parents, to no avail; he has ignored truancy. He has saved the Young Ben from reform school. Under constant pressure from the community, Mr. Digby feels that he can do no more. However, he is to be greatly surprised at the events of the school board meeting, in Chapter 30.

CHAPTER 30

Summary

Mrs. MacMurray, now 82, sat by her open window. Her daughter worried about the draught of the window, but the old woman loved the sights and sounds of the street below. She was waiting for Brian, who never failed to visit her after school. He wanted hockey stockings, which she would knit for him.

Brian brought her the wool. As she knitted, she told him the story of how his grandfather had stared down a bobcat, which he had killed later. Maggie O'Connal entered, rebuking her mother for having the window opened again and for tiring her eyes with knitting. Afterward, the old woman sat alone until dark, wondering what her life meant. It did not make sense to her.

The next day, she continued her knitting, while telling Brian about the early prairie days. When Maggie O'Connal heard her mother coughing, she put her to bed with a mustard plaster on her chest. Mrs. O'Connal telephoned Dr. Svarich, who promised to come over later.

Peter Svarich drove Miss Thompson to the school board meeting. Their wedding had been postponed again, this time at Peter's request. When they reached the town hall, he told his fiancée to marry Mr. Digby. He left her and drove off.

The school board dealt smoothly with trivial matters of business until the chairman, Mr. Thorborn, addressed Mr. Digby, explaining that there were several matters the board wanted to bring to his attention. Mr. Digby, he said, was not strict enough in discipline, associated with undesirable people, such as Mr. Palmer and the Ben, and ought to teach Sunday school. The most important problem, though, Mrs. Abercrombie added, was that of the Young Ben. Mr. Digby replied that the Young Ben was no longer in school. The board members declared that Mr. Digby had no right to act on his own, since the Young Ben was only 14, one year below legal school-leaving age. Mrs. Abercrombie insisted that the board have the Young Ben sent away to a correctional school. When Mr. Digby objected to their plan, Mrs. Abercrombie said that he would have to resign. Digby knew that he had fallen into the trap she had laid so carefully. She did not want him to leave; she wanted the Young Ben in reform school.

The board was then stunned by the intervention of Miss Thompson. She pointed out that Mr. Digby would have to live with his decision if he supported the prosecution of the Young Ben. Moreover, she continued, the whole trouble was caused by the blowing up of the Ben's still in the church basement. Mr. Powelly and Mrs. Abercrombie had been thirsting for revenge. It was not enough that the Ben had been jailed; now they wanted to persecute his son. It was, Miss Thompson stated, in accordance with the cruel and spiteful persecution of the Wong children, which had been undertaken by Mariel at her mother's prompting. Declaring that Mrs. Abercrombie had shown her the terrible evil of a black soul, Miss Thompson offered her resignation and left the meeting. Mr. Digby also left.

Mrs. Abercrombie was filled with indignant rage, but suddenly she had no allies. The board, unwilling to lose two teachers, accepted Mrs. Abercrombie's resignation. When she had left, the men were disappointed. The confrontation with the formidable Mrs. Abercrombie had not been an impressive explosion.

Commentary

The chapter is the end of another act of the morality play. Good has triumphed over evil once more. Miss Thompson and Mr. Digby, representing the compassionate forces that have tried to better the lot of deprived children, have defeated Mrs. Abercrombie and Mr. Powelly, whose bigotry has caused suffering and pain. Of course, the episode is presented with W.O. Mitchell's usual quiet humor. Mrs. Abercrombie's rage is almost comical in its propositions, and the sight of the board members falling over one another in their haste to defy the dragon is an occasion for laughter. Nevertheless, the extent of the injury inflicted by the monstrous spite of Mrs. Abercrombie and Mr. Powelly should not be underestimated.

CHAPTER 31

Summary

Mrs. MacMurray was ill and had to remain in bed. Her chest ached and she coughed frequently. She tried to knit the hockey socks for Brian, but her vision was faulty. He opened the window for her and then tiptoed from the room as she fell asleep.

He took his skates to Milt Palmer for sharpening. While Brian was there, Mr. Digby dropped in. The two men began talking philosophy. Brian was fascinated when they discussed the ideas of the philosopher, Berkeley. Milt was puzzled. According to Berkeley, the whole world was inside. Everything was a bundle of sensations inside the self. What troubled Milt was the problem, then, of who *me* was. Digby explained that *me* was God's idea. Milt was inside God, just as everything else was inside Milt. The conversation excited Brian. He asked Mr. Palmer if he had a "feeling." However, Milt said that he had not. He did not understand what Brian was getting at.

Outside the store, Brian questioned Mr. Digby about the ideas he had heard discussed. If everything was a matter of the senses, the boy said, then some things just would not figure out. Mr. Digby assured him that that was all right. Some things could not be figured out. Brian would know some day, when he was older. Until then, he was on the right track by responding to feeling.

As the snow fell gently, Mrs. MacMurray lay silently sleeping.

Commentary

On the level of plot, the chapter foreshadows the death of Brian's grandmother. Mrs. MacMurray is failing fast, spending more and more time sleeping.

There is, here, also a revival of the theme of Brian's spiritual quest. His boyhood has been filled with a longing to know, with a desire to understand fully the spiritual experiences he has encountered in important moments. The conversation in Milt Palmer's shop is a small step in Brian's journey. In part, it is confirmation for him of God's part in man's life. Man, as Mr. Digby declared in explaining Berkeley, is God's idea. The figuring out of the epiphany experiences in God's idea would have to wait until Brian was older. In the meantime, he would simply have to respond to the feeling, which is real.

CHAPTER 32

Summary

Mrs. MacMurray's death was accepted with quiet sadness. Mr. Stickle wrote her a two-column obituary for the *Times*. Uncle Sean took care of the funeral arrangements.

In a conversation with Maggie, Uncle Sean learned that, influenced by his uncle, Brian intended to go to university to become a "dirt doctor." He would learn to cure the ills of prairie farming. In fact, he had already written a school essay on "Why People Should Raise Cows in Southern Saskatchewan." Uncle Sean asked to read the essay.

Two days later, Brian spoke with Mr. Digby. The boy revealed that he had done a lot of thinking since his grandmother's death. He confessed that he did not think he would experience his special feeling anymore. Digby was struck by the seriousness of the boy's face. It had an expression that reminded him of the strange maturity of the Young Ben. Perhaps, Digby advised the boy, he had already grown up.

Brian entered his grandmother's room. He examined it thoughtfully: the pictures, the abandoned leg brace, the log-cabin quilt. As he looked, a familiar awareness came back to him, an awareness that perhaps had been there only since his father's death. A sense of the long line of death, stretching back through generations, came to him.

Outside, crunching through the snow, he asked himself why people had to die. "It was awful to be human," he concluded. As he responded unwillingly to the beauty of nature around him, the answers to his questions were puzzling. They had something to do with all he had experienced: with dying, and with being born; with loving, and with being hungry; with the prairie; and with the Ben and Mr. Digby. Some day, he decided, he would know.

The day drew to a close, the night air echoing to the cries of animals. The wind drifted over the prairie. The northern lights shone overhead and the town lights gleamed. Day would succeed night, and the years would pass.

Commentary

The final chapter leaves Brian's pilgrimage at a critical stage. He has won through to a kind of maturity. His response to the prairie and his encounters with its people have shaped the course of his life. He will become an agricultural scientist. His life will be devoted to caring for the land he has come to love. It is not an idle or childish decision; his school essay is evidence of his genuine concern. It is a decision that, while it has sprung from his first mystical response to the land, has moved on to a sense of responsibility, of mission.

Brian has also developed spiritually. His early, childish questions about God now have a mature ring to them. He has sensed that those questions are part of the whole problem of being human. Thus, all human experiences prompt the questions and all human experiences suggest the answers. His aspirations are now no longer locked within him as answers to personal puzzles; they are an aspect of the whole world around him. His vision is thus broader and more mature.

Character Sketches

Brian Sean MacMurray O'Connal

The central character in the novel seems in many ways to be an ordinary boy, the kind of boy one might expect to encounter in a small town. His activities are certainly not extraordinary. As a small child, he plays in a sandbox, draws pictures with crayons and is intrigued by commonplace things, such as the sight of porridge bubbling in the pot. When he is older, he skates, swims and plays baseball and hockey. These are definitely not the exploits of a superhero.

He is, though, a dutiful and intelligent boy. In spite of the unfortunate events of his first day at school, when he came into conflict with Miss MacDonald, Brian wants to do well in school. After the first few months, there are explicit indications of his obedience and diligence:

> Brian was a Gopher; Forbsie and Artie were Ants; Mariel Abercrombie was a Grasshopper—Miss Mac-Donald had the children divided into three groups. Brian took great pride in the fact that the Gophers were ahead of the rest of the room in Health. The Gophers chewed their food more and harder than the Ants or the Grasshoppers; they neglected fewer times to sleep with their windows open; they brushed their teeth more religiously. In the matter of vitamins they were slightly behind the Grasshoppers, but they were still ahead on the overall count. (p. 89)

His apparent seriousness about his education is emphasized in the last chapter, when it is revealed that he had decided to become a "dirt doctor." Further, he shoulders his share of responsibilities in the family. When he is very young, he polishes the family shoes on Sunday mornings. Later, he teaches Bobbie to skate and to swim. In fact, his only really thoughtless acts are his stealing of the pillow (Chapter 4), his taking of the pigeon (Chapter 7) and his attempt to drive Uncle Sean's horses (Chapter 25).

Brian is, however, an extremely sensitive boy. That is why he is so distressed by the lack of attention paid to him during his brother's illness and why he reacts with such terror to Miss MacDonald's threats over the hand-washing incident. But his unique sensitivity is revealed in more important things that show it to be a special responsiveness of the heart and spirit. The early magic that possesses him in his first response to nature sets him apart from his peers. Brian is the one who can experience "a soft explosion of feeling" (p. 60). It is he who comes to know "completion" and "culmination." Unlike Art, he understands the abstract concepts of justice and right that are illustrated by the Young Ben's actions in the gopher incident. This special quality of his personality emerges most strongly at the end of the book, when Mr. Digby sees in Brian what the poet Wordsworth called "Intimations of Immortality."

It is a strange irony that such a special quality should be found in an apparently ordinary boy in an ordinary small town. It may be ironic, but it is surely not altogether surprising, for Brian is, to some extent, the product of four major influences in his life: from his father, he inherited love; from his mother, duty; from his grandmother, reverence for the past; and from his Uncle Sean, a passionate love of the land.

Gerald O'Connal

Gerald is a typical O'Connal, having red hair and being more than six feet tall. Since he is 15 years younger than his brother, Sean, it is not surprising that he is different in temperament. Unlike Sean, he is quiet to the point of being shy. Perhaps the difference in temperament is also due, in part, to the fact that he has a university education, whereas Sean has not.

Mr. O'Connal is a successful, hard-working man. He owns the town drugstore. Even though he suffers from a mysterious sleepiness, he refuses, in spite of his wife's urgings, to reduce his hours at the store. His industry has given him a good business and a good home.

Gerald O'Connal is also very much a family man. He helps his wife in caring for their ailing son, Bobbie. In truly paternal fashion, he gives Brian his early lessons in sex education, when the boy is puzzling over the reproduction of pigeons and rabbits. It is worth noting that when Brian's pigeon dies, Mr. O'Connal is the one who takes his son to the prairie to bury the bird.

Kindness and gentleness seem to be his chief characteristics. When Brian runs into trouble after his first day at school, he turns first to his father, whose words are certainly not harsh: "You'll just have to make sure it doesn't happen again." In this episode, Brian's summing-up of his father is revealing:

> Slightly lighter of heart, Brian left the store. It was always easier to explain to his father. With the discernment that children have, Brian and Bobbie had both measured the indulgence of their father. (p. 78)

Mr. O'Connal loves his sons "with a consistently deep emotion" that, he is aware, often makes him "helplessly indulgent." He shows the same kind of steady love for his brother, Sean. He hopes that Brian and Bobbie will grow to know the same kind of bond that exists between Sean and him. Moreover, though he has long since paid back the money that Sean had lent him for his education, he thinks of telling his brother that he still owes him a couple of hundred, so that Sean can finance his irrigation scheme.

Mr. O'Connal dies in Rochester after gall-bladder surgery. It is ironic that Brian and the Young Ben, between whom a mysterious bond exists, should have such different fathers. The Ben is a shifty, irresponsible rogue, whereas Mr. O'Connal is a conscientious, loving parent. It is hardly astonishing that, after his father's death, Brian at times experiences "a faint yearning that sometimes stayed with him throughout an entire day" (p. 251).

Maggie (MacMurray) O'Connal

Maggie was born on a homestead in Saskatchewan. She met her husband during a two-year stay in Ontario with her mother.

She is a slight, pretty woman, with dark hair and eyes, which Brian has inherited. She speaks quickly, with a trace of a Scottish accent in her speech.

Her love for her children is as strong as the love that her husband shows. When Bobbie is sick, she looks after him with skill and love. When Brian has nightmares over the punishment that God metes out to liars, she is anxious and watchful at his bedside. Later, she watches tenderly as the sleeping Brian clutches the tube skates he had wanted so desperately for Christmas.

However, there is an aspect to her character that her husband does not possess. Gerald O'Connal is thankful for the "vein of irony" that is part of his wife's personality:

> In Maggie O'Connal there was a vein of Gaelic "gumption." Unstained by the sin of oversimplifying, she had at an early age arrived at an appreciation of life's complexity and the contrariness of the world's contents, animal, vegetable, mineral, spiritual, and economic. Because there was not in her the slightest trace of conceit, she could not count her chickens before they were hatched; she could not take the easy way with her children. She expected much of them; her punishment seldom went beyond the coolness of disapproval. She had plans for her sons; she wanted them to be as neat as a stooked field, as sweet as a loft of hay, but above all—mature. (p. 78)

She is clearly a woman of firm principle. Thus, when she believes that Miss MacDonald has treated Brian badly, she does not shrink from conflict. She talks to the teacher. Such is the effect of her words that Miss MacDonald, obviously having been made aware of her wrong, decides to change schools.

Maggie O'Connal's ambitions for her sons seem to be coming to fruition in Brian toward the end of the novel; he is planning to obtain a university education. Mr. Digby also notices Brian's unusual maturity at about the same time.

Sean O'Connal

Sean O'Connal, Gerald's older brother, is the liveliest and most passionate man in the O'Connal family.

He stands well over six feet in height, and has "carrot-red" hair and mustache. His pipe smoking incurs the disapproval of his hired man, Ab, and his colorful language is strongly criticized by Mrs. O'Connal and her mother. He operates a farm with help from Ab and from Annie, the housekeeper-cook. He has always been a bachelor and his uncompromising ways are probably the reason for that.

Sean has a very fierce temper. Those who display small-mindedness feel its lash most. For example, when the miserly Bent Candy refuses to help in irrigation schemes, Sean's anger explodes. He will see Candy in hell, he declares. His curses are eloquent and fiery:

> 'We'll both be there!' cried Sean as he started his car.
> 'Ye will be there, bumpin' an' bouncin' an' jigglin' fer
> all eternity with a red-hot tractor seat to shrivel yer
> hide to everlastin'! We'll both be there!' (p. 212)

As might be expected, the penny-pinching banker, Mr. Abercrombie, is also the target of Sean's wrath. When Abercrombie refuses a loan to start the irrigation scheme, Sean's denunciation is impressive:

> 'An' what you say is stupid!' roared Sean. 'Threefold
> stupid for threefold stupid reasons! A—hen manure!
> B—heifer dust! C—buffalo chips!' (p. 81)

And yet Sean is a kind and generous man. In the earlier years, he lent Gerald money for his education. Later, he is quick to offer to look after Brian, when the O'Connals have to travel to Rochester. Every spring and summer after Gerald's death, he drives the O'Connals to visit the grave on Sundays. Toward the end of the novel, having learned of Brian's desire to be a "dirt doctor," he suggests that the boy stay with him in the summer. He is clearly a charitable, thoughtful man, even though he is not a churchgoer. Gerald, Maggie and Mrs. MacMurray go to the Presbyterian Church regularly; Sean does not. He is not religious in a formal sense, but he reveals a true, Christian heart.

Sean is not simply sound and fury, however. Under all the bluster, there are strong indications of a shrewd, thoughtful mind that understands the responsibilities of farming and accepts them with conviction. He is described, for example, as "the keeper of the Lord's vineyard." He sees that Prairie problems stem from two causes: ignorance and neglect. The farmers must battle the prairie winds by turning to strip-farming, and they must solve the problems of drought by means of irrigation projects. So far, they have shown neither the imagination nor the zeal to apply those remedies. In fact, they are neglectful and irresponsible, in Sean's view, because they exploit the land and, then, having reaped the rewards, they depart on vacations to faraway places. That Sean is right in his schemes is demonstrated by the success of his garden.

Mrs. MacMurray

Mrs. MacMurray, the widow of John MacMurray, is Maggie O'Connal's mother and Brian's grandmother. A dignified Scottish woman with a strong sense of good manners, she had been a homesteader in Saskatchewan with her husband. After her husband's death, she apparently went to live in Ontario. A year after her daughter had married Gerald O'Connal, she moved west to live with the new family. She is about 75 years old when the novel opens, and is 82 when she dies, seemingly from old age and pneumonia.

She is a woman with very strong Presbyterian convictions about proper conduct. Thus, she disapproves vocally of Sean's rough ways and coarse language. Moreover, her death is a reflection of her attitudes, as the novelist points out with gentle humor: "She managed a departure typically Scotch and Presbyterian in its restraint, a predestined event of logical finality. In her own words, her time had come" (p. 295). To the end, her appreciation of decorum is apparent.

Nevertheless, she is a caring, kindly woman. She assumes much of the responsibility for running the household during Bobbie's illness. She welcomes Brian's visits to her room after school and feeds him chocolates from a box in her drawer. She makes clothes for him; she is busy knitting him a pair of hockey stockings when she dies.

Her close relationship with Brian is significant. He seems to have inherited from the MacMurray side of the family a strong sense of moral values. That strong moral conscience is displayed in his terror at having told a lie and in his reaction to the Young Ben during the gopher incident. But Mrs. MacMurray contributes more than moral sensitivity. Her tales of early homesteading days surely feed Brian's imagination. She creates, as it were, the myths about the land that later help to give birth to his idea of becoming a "dirt doctor." She is, then, a formative influence on her grandson.

The Young Ben

The Young Ben is, without doubt, one of the strangest characters in Canadian fiction. Never referred to by his first name, he appears and reappears in the novel with spiritlike silence. He does not speak a single word and he has no friends apart from his puzzling closeness with Brian.

His father, the still-operator, boasting about his illegitimate children in the beer parlor, gives an unusual account of his son's birth and ends by declaring emphatically, "Thuh goddam kid was borned growed-up." There is, indeed, a remarkable maturity in the boy that all of his teachers notice. But none of them is able to handle him. He is disinterested in school (he spends three years in Grade 1), and his persistent truancy finally obliges Mr. Digby to remove him from the roll. However, the Young Ben's maturity has nothing to do with school.

He is, above all, somehow symbolic of an aspect of the prairie. Even before Brian knows who the boy is, he identifies the Young Ben with the prairie. "This is your prairie," Brian says in Chapter 1. His attributes are attributes that are part of the prairie, as Miss Thompson comes to understand:

> The Young Ben played no games with the other children; he did not bother with agates in marble season, and would take no part in organized team games. He could run with the swiftness of a prairie chicken, Miss Thompson found out from Brian O'Connal; he could jump like an antelope; but he could not be interested in races or Field Day competitions. School was an intolerable incarceration for him, made bearable only by flights of freedom which totalled up to almost the same number as did the days he attended. (p. 147)

Since the prairie is associated in the novel with revelation of the divine, the Young Ben is clearly related to good qualities. He certainly does not lack, for example, a sense of moral indignation. When Brian is punished harshly by Miss MacDonald, the Young Ben moves threateningly to protect the young boy. On the prairie, he deals out swift justice to Art, who has cruelly mistreated a gopher. However, the Young Ben's morality is by no means conventional. Thus, wanting a gun and ammunition, he simply steals what he desires from the hardware store.

His values are the values of the untouched prairie. Like the prairie, he is everywhere, enduring and silent, indifferent to the feverish, materialistic notions that haunt the inhabitants of the town. It is appropriate that Brian, identifying his quest for understanding with the prairie, should recognize in the Young Ben a fellow soul, one who does understand, though the understanding is never articulated. Roaming the prairie, the Young Ben has found, in his own strange fashion, the answers to the philosophical questions that plague Mr. Hislop, Mr. Digby and Milt Palmer.

Saint Sammy

Sammy Belterlaben, known as Saint Sammy in the novel, is not a major character in the conventional sense. In fact, he appears in the narrative only two or three times. He nevertheless makes a major contribution in terms of theme, and for that reason he deserves close scrutiny.

He began, before the novel opens, as a farmer on a place owned by somebody called Horn. His work was a failure, and droughts ruined him. Now, having received a revelation from God, he has taken his animals—notably, his Clydesdale horses— and gone to live in a piano box on Magnus Petersen's land. There he lives as the novel opens, collecting underwear labels, matchboxes, bits of stone and twigs, and other odds and ends in a battered tin box, and calling down God's vengeance against Bent Candy and the wayward town. Bent Candy is, of course, his archenemy, for Candy covets the Clydesdales and will go to any lengths to have them for himself.

Sammy is a figure obviously associated with the prairie. Yet he is completely unlike the other two prairie figures, Brian and the Young Ben. In their association with nature, they suggest a communion of joy or an alliance with immutable forces. Sammy sees the prairie as the perfect kingdom of God, which man has sullied and marred. It was Eden, but man spoiled it.

Thus, he now seems to view the prairie as the arena in which God will exact punishment. He is proved right. Bent Candy's new barn is demolished by a storm that Sammy seems to summon. Whether, in fact, the storm has been his messenger is impossible to say. It is hardly likely that Mitchell meant the incident to have that moral. Seeing it as a happy and rather amusing coincidence would appear to be a more sensible interpretation. Whatever the answer is, the fact remains that Sammy is not really an important influence on Brian. He is intrigued by the man's eccentricity, but Sammy does not arouse Brian's "special feeling," except for the fact that he is carried away by the "fervor" of the old man's words. When Sammy later has his hour of triumph, Brian feels excitement, but the event brings no epiphany.

Sammy is, above all, probably a reminder of God's demands, demands cutting across human concerns. In this function, he is one of the three characters in the novel who are closely associated with the prairie. It is entertaining to consider the notion that the three represent the three different aspects of God: the Father who disciplines (Sammy); the Son who is love (Brian); and the Spirit who is everywhere (the Young Ben).

James Digby

James Digby is the principal of the town's public school. He is a rather lean, ungainly man, who is 38 years old when Miss Thompson arrives. Though he does not have a university degree, he is thoughtful and scholarly. He has philosphical conversations with Mr. Hislop, and he encourages Milt Palmer's reading by exchanging books with him.

He is revealed as a sensitive and compassionate person. When, on the first day of school, Miss MacDonald drags Brian to him, the principal dismisses the teacher by observing that she should return to her class and let them go home. He also responds sympathetically to Mr. Hislop's plight in the conflict with Mrs. Abercrombie and the church elders. He stands by the minister and puts an arm around his shoulder. Nowhere is his compassion seen more vividly than in his protection of the Young Ben. In spite of the awkward situation it creates for him, he ignores the boy's truancy. At last, facing the facts of the situation, he simply drops the boy from the roll. Digby is also instrumental, with Miss Thompson and Dr. Svarich, in trying to help the Wong family. He offers to pay half their grocery bill.

Digby is an intelligent man, with a considerable understanding of life. On the first day of school, he wants to explain to Brian what the school is trying to do. He wants to explain, though he realizes the impossibility of doing so, that everyone is an individual "whose every emotion, wish, action, was the resultant of two forces: what he felt and truly wanted, what he thought he should feel and ought to want" (p. 73). He wanted, in other words, to give the boy "the faiths that belonged to all other men."

His shrewd intelligence emerges in his conversations with Milt Palmer. When Milt is discouraged by his reading of philosophy and is ready to give up thinking altogether, Digby's argument is persuasive:

> So you're not a tree—a tree can be a tree without thinking—it's a good tree when it's growing without thinking. A shoemaker, on the other hand, is an animal—uh—with the right number and kind of guts—that has to think some to be a shoemaker; if he doesn't think, he's not a good man or a shoemaker. (p. 137)

At the end of the novel, he is the one who expresses most explicitly the different quality in Brian. He recognizes the new-found maturity and links it with the same quality in the Young Ben.

There is, however, a slightly comic aspect to Mr. Digby. That is seen most vividly after Miss Thompson arrives in town. He is immediately enchanted by her and quickly calculates the age difference between them. Though he is usually careless about his appearance, wearing his only pair of shoes until they are falling apart, he sets about improving himself. When he is hopelessly in love with Miss Thompson, the picture of him is amusing in the distress it conveys:

> He alternately cursed and blessed the fact that he and Miss Thompson worked together. When he was not with her, he could hardly wait for the candid and

temperate friendship of her company; when he was with her on school business, he wished with all his heart that the woman were a thousand miles away. The smell of her hair, the casual touch of her arm, simply the nearness of her, were torture. He wished that the school term would hurry its end; he wished that the school term would never finish. With spring and blandishing chinooks, he became, for the first time in his teaching career, irritable and unreasonable. When he himself realized it, he went down to Milt Palmer's, talked philosophy, drank the Ben's brew, and got very drunk. (p. 254)

Above all else, James Digby functions in the narrative as a champion of goodness and compassion. In a conversation about the Young Ben, he exposes Mr. Powelly's hypocrisy mercilessly. At the end, he is no less unyielding before Mrs. Abercrombie. Though not a churchgoer, he knows true values and champions their cause.

Ruth Thompson

Miss Thompson, the new teacher, is a young woman of 26 or 27. She has dark hair and large, brown eyes. Digby noticed particularly "the sudden expressiveness of her face" and "the girlish quality of excitement in her" (p. 131).

She has taught for eight years: three years in a community called Westward and five years in Azure. It was in Azure that she met Peter Svarich, to whom she had become engaged. She had ended that engagement, and there is, at first, some discomfort in returning to a community in which Svarich has his practice. When she comes to town, she stays in a cottage with Miss Taylor, who works at the telephone office, and Miss James, who works at Blaine's store.

Ruth Thompson is an uncompromising individualist with firm convictions. In her classroom, her manner is kind but firm. In her relationship with Peter Svarich, her character shows itself clearly. She had broken off the engagement in Azure because of Peter's attitude. He was ashamed of his Ukrainian parentage and, in compensation, his behavior could be unnecessarily assertive. When their relationship is resumed, she becomes aware that he has not changed. She realizes that "the key to Peter was his need for respect and attention." He demands too much of her. As a result, she makes a strong claim for her own individuality:

> You know—I'm an individual too. I'm not you, Peter. I'm another person with feelings and wants and thoughts. You can't have all of me. (p. 257)

Not surprisingly, the new engagement, like the first, is broken off. Ruth cannot compromise herself.

Miss Thompson emerges as a compassionate person with a dislike of intolerance. Her work on behalf of the Wong family is a dramatic illustration of her beliefs. She reprimands Mariel Abercrombie for her unkind treatment of the Wong children. She is blunt and forthright with Mayor Neally about what she regards as the town's neglect of the Wongs' situation. She also arranges with Mr. Digby to pay half the Wongs' grocery bill, though she finds later that Svarich has already paid it.

Most of all, Miss Thompson functions in the novel, along with Digby, as a champion for good in the town. In fact, she is the one who is finally most responsible for the defeat of Mrs. Abercrombie. At the school board meeting in Chapter 30, she criticizes the trustees for their hypocrisy in their persecution of the Ben, exposing Mr. Powelly's unwholesome influence in that scheme. She is even more merciless with Mrs. Abercrombie, describing her as "insensitive," "vindictive" and "wicked." The teacher's words are as blunt as they are accurate: "Tonight you've shown me the heart of darkness—you, Mrs. Abercrombie! It is in you—all of it—in your dark, dark soul!"

Mrs. Abercrombie

Mrs. Abercrombie is a large, imposing woman who is the principal exponent of wickedness in the town. Her involvement in good causes is impressive: "She was active in church work, the Red Cross, Daughters of the Empire, the Eastern Star, the library board, the local relief committee for the unfortunates of the dried-out area" (p. 46). However, in all of her good works, her vanity and her insensitivity are dominant.

Her vanity is unmistakable. She wears several expensive

rings on her fingers and is inordinately proud of "the dignity of her husband's work" and "a trip they had taken to Europe six years before."

Mrs. Abercrombie sings in the church choir and works closely with the minister, but her actions are completely uncharitable. She is responsible for Mr. Hislop's resignation over the trivial question of the use of candles in the church, but her real grievance lay in the minister's Christian concern for Romona (p. 25). Her bigotry is displayed in forbidding Mariel to attend the Wongs' birthday party. Nowhere is her wickedness more vividly displayed, however, than in her persecution, with Mr. Powelly, of the Bens. It is a source of some comfort that the school trustees finally turn on her, accepting a resignation she did not mean to offer.

Structure

As soon as the reader is able to distinguish between the objective, factual reporting of an event and an artist's rendering of the same event, the concept of the plot is born. The distinction may be seen, in its most basic form, in the difference between an entry in a biographical dictionary and a short story about the life of the same person. The entry in the biographical dictionary is straightforward reporting. Facts are assembled and, without any embellishment by the editor, recorded in chronological order. The treatment of the same facts in a story is quite different. In that case, the writer adds interpretation and shapes the information about the man in order to make some point of significance. The biographical dictionary presents a record; the story offers meaning. In seeking to accomplish his task, the writer has to shape his narrative. He highlights some episodes and perhaps omits others altogether. That shaping is what is meant by plot.

Thus, a distinction must be made between story and plot. A story, in the words of the eminent critic and novelist, E.M. Forster, may be only "a narrative of events arranged in their time sequence." A straight adventure story, with its emphasis upon each exciting event as it happens, would fall into the category of story. However, *Who Has Seen The Wind* is in a different category. It is much more sophisticated; it does not merely unfold the story of Brian O'Connal's childhood. W.O. Mitchell has sophisticated concerns, so his novel deals with meanings: the nature of human beings, the complexity of human society, the responsibilities inherent in being human and the puzzling relationship between the spiritual and the material in human life.

To accomplish his purposes, Mitchell has fashioned a carefully crafted plot structure. That structure helps to illuminate what he has to say to his readers. We will examine plot structure in terms of Dramatic Structure, Epiphanies and the symbols of The Prairie and The Wind.

Dramatic Structure

The novel has four parts, each of which can be seen as a

kind of act in the plot. Each part deals with about two years in Brian's life and has its own atmosphere and organization.

Part I opens with Brian at four years of age. His activities and concerns in this section are, appropriately, typical of childhood: exploring the town, playing with friends, crayoning a picture of God, trying to make something with pillow feathers, disliking carrots for dinner and wondering how pigeons came to be born. At this period of his life, Brian is not greatly troubled by adult concerns. His quest for knowledge of God is very much a child's quest.

In this part of the novel, Mitchell's emphasis on more serious questions comes only sporadically. The beginning of Brian's spiritual seeking is only the experience of a moment. It comes in his first encounter with the Young Ben, at the end of Chapter 1. But the shaping of the first section is actually directed toward the focus in Chapter 7. At that point, Brian has had his first brush with death, the death of the pigeon. As a result, his responses are more explicit. Now, his feelings are closely associated with the prairie, where he was entranced by "soft and distant explosions of light" from the prairie thunderstorm. Not surprisingly, two days later, Brian, feeling a sense of life's beauty and goodness, has an experience that is described as "a soft explosion of feeling." The nature of Brian's experiences is thus clearer. What he feels is related to the prairie, and the prairie has already been associated with God. Obviously, his special feeling has some relation to the divine presence. There is no element of the intellectual in his response. He gets where he is at the end of the first section by feeling, not reason, certainly appropriate for a boy of four. Part I has clearly been shaped to stress Brian's developing spirituality.

Part I also acts as an introduction to a second major aspect of the novel, social criticism. Mr. Hislop loses his battle with Mrs. Abercrombie and the church elders. A scholarly and devout man, he is obliged to leave the town. That event is a prelude to the more wicked deeds yet to come. As a prelude, it is a foreshadowing of the conflict in the town between charity and bigotry. The antagonists are clearly to be Mr. Digby and Mrs. Abercrombie in the course of a conflict that is an ironic backdrop to Brian's spiritual search.

The final aspect of shaping in Part I is noteworthy. The

novel opens by emphasizing the immenseness of the prairie, "the least common denominator of nature, the skeleton requirements simply, of land and sky." Chapter 7, the last of the section, focusses attention on the same environment, with a haunting picture of the insignificance of man against the vast silence of the prairie:

> Shadows lengthen; the sunlight fades from cloud to cloud, kindling their torn edges as it dies from softness to softness down the prairie sky. A lone farmhouse window briefly blazes; the prairie bathes in mellower, yellower light, and the sinking sun becomes a low and golden glowing on the prairie's edge.
>   Leaning slightly backward against the reins looped round his waist, a man walks homeward from the fields. The horses' heads move gently up and down; their hoofs drop tired sound; the jingling of the traces swinging at their sides is clear against the evening hush. The stubble crackles; a killdeer calls. Stooks, fences, horses, man, have clarity that was not theirs throughout the day. (p. 61)

The implication of the two passages is plain: the story is to be acted out against a background that is eternal. Man is troubled, and his actions are attempts to deal with his troubles. Nature, in contrast, is immutable and all-encompassing.

As Part II opens, Brian is six years old. As a sign that he is older, his activities have changed. He now goes to school. He learns to skate. He goes gopher hunting on the prairie.

There is still naïveté in his response to the message of nature. He experiences "a growing elation of such fleeting delicacy and poignancy that he dared not turn his mind to it for fear that he might spoil it." The experience prompted by the sight of the spirea leaf has the same quality of sensual delight that was apparent earlier in the novel:

> A twinkling of light caught his eye; and he turned his head to see that the new, flake leaves of the spirea were starred in the sunshine—on every leaf were drops that had gathered during the night. He got up. They

lay limpid, cradled in the curve of the leaves, each with a dark lip of shadow under its curving side and a star's cold light in its pure heart. As he bent more closely over one, he saw the veins of the leaf magnified under the perfect crystal curve of the drop. The barest breath of a wind stirred at his face, and its caress was part of the strange enchantment too. (p. 107)

His initial response is innocent and childlike. However, as this part unfolds, the experience becomes more complex. The events of the gopher hunt, the sight of the two-headed calf and the death of Jappy all add puzzling aspects to Brian's growing up. By the time Part II closes, Brian's response to existence has changed; the innocent boy has become aware of the clouds of experience that hover over the days of man. His joy is chastened. His feelings are more sober. Now, "something was gone . . . Now there was an emptiness that wasn't to be believed" (p. 181).

In a similar fashion, the subplot in Part II becomes more complex. The forces of social injustice, led by Mrs. Abercrombie and Mr. Powelly, have emerged with greater definition and vigor. They are responsible for the hounding of the Ben and for the tragic fate of the Wong family. In opposition, Mr. Digby and Miss Thompson become heroic figures. The evil has not halted, but there is a strong foreshadowing of the areas of conflict yet to come.

At the beginning of Part III, Brian is eight years old. He has begun to swear. He experiments with smoking cigarettes. He is old enough to stay at Uncle Sean's farm. He tries to drive the horses. He runs away from the farm. Clearly, he has, in a chronological sense, grown up in the two years that have passed.

However, in addition, his spiritual understanding is seen to have matured. When the old feeling of excitement returns to him, it is no longer pure, unadulterated, sensual delight. An intellectual element has appeared. Reacting to Saint Sammy's religious ramblings, Brian says, "It wouldn't be so bad . . . if a person knew, or even knew what it was that he wanted to know." True, he is then "alive as he had never been before," but the experiences escape "the grasp of his understanding" (p. 199). This maturer Brian is thus much more able to grapple with the problem of the runt pig and the dilemma of Annie's eye. He comes to the conclusion, in both of those episodes, that he must simply accept the imperfection of what exists. The conclusion is reached as the result of a rational process.

Consequently, at the end of Part III, Brian is able to deal with the most shattering blow of all: the death of his father. That calamity is not met with mere feeling; there is, first, understanding and, second, action. Brian comes to understand and accept the reality of human mortality: "People were forever born; people forever died, and never were again" (p. 246). Things are "different now." As a result, Brian does not lose himself in the luxury of his feelings, as he might have done two years earlier, and certainly would have done four years earlier. He makes a decision. He turns toward his mother and the responsibilities that lie with his family. The shape of the novel has been dramatically fashioned by the shaping of Brian's understanding.

Similarly, the subplot is brought into sharper focus in Part III. The evil forces are bending their energies toward a single target: the Bens. The machinations of the evildoers lead directly to the dramatic denouement in the final section of the novel.

In Part IV, Brian is almost 11. Older now, he teaches Bobbie to skate and to swim. He plays baseball and hockey. He has long talks with his grandmother. He is evidently growing up and has developed an appropriate sense of his responsibility. In keeping with his developing nature, he decides to become a "dirt doctor."

Brian's spiritual vision also reflects greater maturity. At the beginning of this section, he reveals that in the past two years he has seldom thought of "the yearning that had harried him as long as he could remember" (p. 252). Even a visit to Saint Sammy, "for the express purpose of recapturing the feeling," does not work. Later, the visitation of Sammy's judgment upon Bent Candy causes Brian excitement, but that event has none of the feeling of earlier epiphanies. After his grandmother dies, however, Brian does enter a new stage of his development. The experience is prompted, in part, by the intellectual discussion between Mr. Digby and Milt Palmer, who discuss the problem of "me" and its relationship to God. As a result, when Mr. Digby meets Brian, he notices a change in the boy. He detects in

Brian "maturity in spite of the formlessness of childish features, wisdom without years" (p. 297). Thus, the final section of the novel moves coherently toward the climactic vision with which it ends: the assurance Brian finds in his acceptance of human mortality.

The subplot also moves to a denouement in the fourth part. Mrs. Abercrombie's machinations are exposed publicly and she is defeated in an open battle. The Bens are safe, for the time being, at least, and the children of the town are being taught by Mr. Digby and Miss Thompson, people of charitable vision and good heart.

Epiphanies

In examining the structure of *Who Has Seen The Wind*, it is evident that Brian's experiences of epiphany—those moments of special insight and awareness that he knows throughout his childhood—provide a unifying thread that binds the narrative together.

As is clear from the full exposition in the section of these *Notes* dealing with structure, those moments of epiphany develop in complexity and significance as the story unfolds. It is unnecessary, at this point, to analyze them in detail. It is important, however, to perceive clearly the progression in these special moments and to understand how each is linked to a stage of Brian's development. The thread is easily discernible:

First Epiphany:	Chapter 1	the majesty of the prairie
Second Epiphany:	Chapter 7	the death of the pigeon
Third Epiphany:	Chapter 12	the spirea leaf
Fourth Epiphany:	Chapter 14	the gopher
Fifth Epiphany:	Chapter 20	the two-headed calf
Sixth Epiphany:	Chapter 26	Mr. O'Connal's death
Seventh Epiphany:	Chapter 32	human mortality

The epiphanies are a significant aspect of the themes of the novel, and they also contribute to the dramatic structure. In addition, they can be seen as forming a motif that aids the development of the plot, since they illustrate powerfully Brian's progression from a state of naïve innocence to a way of thinking that is more mature and profound.

The Prairie and The Wind

Both of these elements of setting are discussed extensively elsewhere in these *Notes*. It is useful to emphasize, however, that both elements are more than mere aspects of the setting.

The prairie and the wind are, in a significant way, factors in the structure of the novel. It is not by accident, for example, that the narrative opens and closes with a sweeping survey of the prairie landscape. The inference is easily understood: the land, indeed the whole of nature, is the eternal background against which the lives of mortals are acted out. Men are born and die, but the world of God is eternal, as Brian learns. Thus, the prairie and the wind are constants in all of the events that take place. These elements make their appearance in every part of the novel and, therefore, act as a unifying force in the structure.

Themes

Brian's Development

Who Has Seen The Wind is basically the story of a boy growing up. The novel follows the life of Brian O'Connal, a boy living in a small, Saskatchewan prairie town, from the age of four to the age of 11. On the level of bare narrative, it is not a dramatic story. There are no bloody wars or violent revolutions to shatter the peace, nor are there any exceptional heroes to amaze the reader with dazzling exploits. In fact, in some ways it is a commonplace story. Brian plays the usual childhood games, makes the usual childhood friendships, goes to school and learns, day by day, more of the world in which he lives. The experiences he has to deal with are the experiences of most children: the fear of the first day at school; the death of a pet bird; experimenting with smoking cigarettes; finding out about the mysteries of sex; the death of a parent. Thus, he grows up in much the same way as most boys in a small town might have in the 1920s and 1930s. His world is, on the surface, ordinary.

However, there is a dimension to Brian's growing up that adds a distinctly different element to the novel. That element lies in Mitchell's endeavor to reveal to us the process of Brian's intellectual and spiritual development. Brian does not simply grow older and follow more manly pursuits; he becomes more mature. He does not simply do things; he learns. He does not simply become less childish; he changes as a person.

Thus, the most important theme in the book is Brian's intellectual and spiritual growth, for the novel is essentially a story of initiation into manhood. Although the process is not completed before the novel ends, Brian, the child, does become Brian, the man, to a large degree. At first, he appears as a true child of innocence, delighting in the beauty and mystery of his environment. In the years that follow, he is faced by a number of events that challenge his thoughts and emotions. Finally, by the end of the novel, he has become the child of experience, a person who has won his way through to a special kind of maturity. The three stages of that development deserve careful study.

1. Brian as the Child of Innocence

At the age of four, when the novel begins, Brian's knowledge of the world is necessarily limited. The most important factor in his existence is the illness of his baby brother, Bobbie. That illness prompts Brian to feel frustrated and resentful. His parents, worried and preoccupied, are not paying attention to him. His grandmother, in Brian's view, is irritable and officious. He is often told to be quiet or is sent out to play. Brian's reaction is to imagine the punishment that God will deal out to his grandmother. He is obviously judging the world from the typical egocentric position of a four-year-old, with no understanding of the grave crisis his family faces. Brian's world is small; it encompasses only Brian's family and Brian's emotions.

Brian's first experience of the prairie reveals the same innocent response. He responds spontaneously, with his senses. It is idyllic, a wonderland of sights and sounds that he has not known before:

> The hum of telephone wires along the road, the ring of hidden crickets, the stitching sound of grasshoppers, the sudden relief of a meadow lark's song, were deliciously strange to him. (p. 11)

In that moment, Brian and his environment are one. He is man untouched by knowledge of sin, and his world is God's creation untouched by ugliness. In the same innocent, idealistic spirit, he imagines himself, in Chapter 4, riding the vacuum cleaner "all the way past the poplars to the clouds—God's clouds where it was blue and sunshiny." When he draws a picture of God, the portrait uses all the brightest colors of his crayons: blue, yellow, green, purple and red. They are as bright as the colors the sunshine cast into the house, when "from the high den window dropped staining light, the bevelled glass breaking it up into violet, blue and red." God and His world are one in their beauty, and it is a beauty to which the boy's senses respond with unequivocal delight.

2. Brian's Formative Experiences

Brian's responses do not remain unspoiled for long. As

time passes, he encounters experiences that demand reflection, and each encounter changes him to some degree.

His first lesson is an experience of death and sadness. It occurs after Brian has been obliged to give his dog, Jappy, temporarily to the Hoffmans because of the animal's wild behavior in the O'Connal house. Lonely without his pet, Brian secretly takes a baby pigeon from the Hoffmans' loft. To his surprise, the bird dies. Brian sheds his first tears of sorrow. Puzzled, he asks his father why the pigeon died. The reply is no explanation. "It happens to things," Mr. O'Connal tells him. The small boy finds some consolation in burying the bird out on his beloved prairie, where a distant lightning storm signals Brian's first faltering step on the path of experience. However, he is not yet, by any means, fully initiated into the wisdom of experience. In spite of the sadness that has come to him through the mystery of death, Brian retains his joyous innocence. Two days later, reunited with his puppy, he lies under a hedge at the side of the house. Here, his sense of harmony with the world around him returns:

> The puppy whimpered slightly in its sleep; it nudged its head further into Brian's neck. The boy was aware that the yard was not still. Every grass-blade and leaf and flower seemed to be breathing, or perhaps, whispering—something to him—something for him. The puppy's ear was inside out. Within himself, Brian felt a soft explosion of feeling. It was one of completion and of culmination. (p. 60)

Brian's second lesson is an encounter with terror in Chapter 10. He is a dutiful, obedient boy, but he tells his teacher, Miss MacDonald, that he has washed his hands and face before coming to school, when in fact he has not done so. The teacher metes out excessive punishment, forcing him to stand before the class with his hands stretched out. More important, she terrifies the boy with threats of God's punishment for liars. So shocked is Brian by the incident that he is ill for two days. He has frightening nightmares about an avenging God pursuing him, so that "panic lifted within him, subsided, rose again and washed over him till he trembled unmercifully and sweat started out over his entire body." It is true that "the frightening conception of an avenging God" gradually gives way to "a friendlier image." Nevertheless, he cannot return to his earlier naïvete. God can no longer be thought of—to use Brian's vocabulary—as entirely "sunshiny" anymore:

> God could be like a flame, Brian was thinking, not a real flame, but like a flame. Perhaps He was a great person made entirely of flame—with a flame beard and flame lips licking out to change the shape of His mouth. For a moment he thought that the old terror was going to wash over him. He should not have thought of that. (p. 99)

The third experience that helps to shape the pattern of Brian's intellectual and spiritual development occurs in Chapter 14, when Brian, Bobbie, Art and Fat go gopher hunting. Their hunt is successful, as one squeaking gopher runs in terror from its burrow. In an act of boyish cruelty, Art picks up the frightened animal and, holding it by the tail, whirls it round his head before finally flinging it to the ground with a thump. Suddenly, the Young Ben, who "had come upon them without a sound," springs into action. He puts the gopher out of its misery swiftly and then administers a merciless beating to Art. The effect on Brian is dramatic. To him, the Young Ben is an intrinsic part of the prairie, as natural in that environment as a coyote. Thus, the prairie boy triggers in Brian the resurgence of the special feeling that he has previously known in moments of communion with nature. In this particular moment, a new element in Brian's response appears. He now experiences a sense of the moral rightness of things. Nature is no longer simply a realm of beauty and sensual grandeur; it is a kingdom in which there is moral law:

> And Brian, quite without any desire to alleviate Art's suffering, shaken by his discovery that the Young Ben was linked in some indefinable way with the magic that visited him often now, was filled with a sense of the justness, the rightness, the completeness of what the

Young Ben had done—what he himself would like to have done. (pp. 127-128)

The "magic" is no longer an innocent communion of feeling; it has developed an aspect of moral awareness. The experience is completed some time later, when Brian and Bobbie, walking on the prairie, come across the decaying body of the gopher. The sight is ugly. The body is covered with "black bits of ants" and is surrounded by a "cloud of flies." "It was difficult," Brian thought, "to believe that this thing had once been a gopher that ran and squeaked over the prairie." The familiar feeling rises within Brian, but now it has "a new, frightening quality." There comes to him a sense of the inscrutable nature of God, who rules over all creatures with awesome power:

Prairie's awful, thought Brian, and in his mind there loomed vaguely fearful images of a still and brooding spirit, a quiescent power unsmiling from everlasting to everlasting to which the coming and passing of the prairie's creatures was but incidental. (pp. 128-129)

The "intensely blue sky" remains, reminiscent of Brian's earlier thoughts of God's "sunshiny" kingdom, but the vision is now much more somber. The glow of innocence is more subdued; the shadows of experience have appeared.

This change is best understood in the light of Brian's earlier vision (in Chapter 12) of the spirea leaf. Then, the sight of "the new, flake leaves of the spirea . . . starred in the sunshine" aroused a "strange enchantment" in Brian. He was filled with "a growing elation of such fleeting delicacy and poignancy that he dared not turn his mind to it for fear that he might spoil it." That experience was an experience of feeling unadulterated by reflection. In contrast, the gopher incident is a moment of moral awareness.

The episode of the two-headed calf in Chapter 20 is the prelude to the next stage in Brian's development. Brian and Fat visit Thorborn's Livery Stable, where they hear that there is a two-headed calf inside. With boyish excitement, they hurry to view the animal. It is dead, but it did indeed have two heads, its necks "like a slingshot." Brian is appalled. The creature does not belong in the world he knows; it should not be a part of the scheme of things. His conclusion is simple and definite: "It was wrong!" Clearly, in this moment Brian's concept of a perfect created world has been offended.

The vision of the spirea leaf "under the perfect crystal curve of the drop" of morning dew expressed precisely his earlier conception of the world. The sight of the two-headed calf, however, says something quite different; it declares that there is imperfection in nature. That is a lesson for Brian. The world is the same, but it has a complexity that Brian had not known before. That complexity visits Brian with full force in an event that comes with startling swiftness: the death of his beloved Jappy under the wheels of Joe Pivott's dray. Brian is shattered by the death of his dog. It drains him of feeling, the feeling of excitement and enchantment he had known previously when, for example, he had lain under the hedge with his pet. Now he is quite different:

> Somewhere within Brian something was gone; ever since the accident it had been leaving him as the sand of an hourglass threads away grain by tiny grain. Now there was an emptiness that wasn't to be believed. (p. 181)

What has left Brian is the enchantment. The two-headed calf had puzzled him with its suggestion of an imperfect world. The death of Jappy demonstrates the reality of that imperfection in action.

The fifth stage of Brian's development shows his learning to cope with the apprehension of imperfection. This stage occurs in Chapter 24 during Brian's stay with his Uncle Sean. The first part of it is the episode with the runt pig. The pig is sickly and misshapen. Uncle Sean and Ab want to kill it, and Brian is horrified. After two spankings, he is allowed to keep the pig on condition that he looks after it. However, he has a lesson to learn. The lesson is, quite simply, that no amount of care and feeding will change the runt. Its imperfection must be accepted; it will always be sickly and misshapen. The boy does, in fact, come to that acceptance, which he had not been able to feel when he saw the two-headed calf:

> By the back porch where the runt pig lived in its apple-box home, Brian looked down. It would always be a runt, he decided, a shivery runt. It had no twist to its tail; it would never have. The world was a funny place.
> (p. 229)

The same lesson of acceptance is learned with people, when Brian decides to try to encourage a marriage between Ab and Annie. He decides that the only reason for Ab's not proposing to Annie is the ugly cast in her right eye. He helps her to obtain new spectacles, which solve the problem. Annie's eye is straight again. However, Ab's reaction stuns Brian. Ab shows "a strange coolness" to Annie; he treats her "as though she had been stricken with some terribly contagious disease." Then the truth dawns on the boy; Ab has accepted Annie as she was, cast and all, and the straight eye has changed her in a way that he does not approve of. When she throws the spectacles away, Ab proposes marriage. Brian had been mistaken when he had intervened in a relationship, seeking to perfect it by removing an imperfection. Consequently, he had to learn Ab's kind of acceptance of things as they are.

3. The Final Stage

The death of Brian's father is the most important event in the boy's pilgrimage toward intellectual and spiritual maturity. The death hits him hard. He had felt drained and empty of feeling when Jappy died, but now his response is much more intense. He feels a terrible kind of loneliness:

> He walked on with the tall prairie grass hissing against his legs, out into the prairie's stillness and loneliness that seemed to flow around him, to meet itself behind him, ringing him and separating him from the town.
> (p. 245)

In his agony, he seeks a kindred spirit; he goes to the prairie. He leaves the town, with its feverish intrigues and troubles, for the prairie, which has fed his visions of beauty and peace. At first, the help he receives there is not vastly different from the vision he received on encountering the remains of the dead gopher. Then, he was shocked by the ugliness of death and the indifference of the prairie. The gopher, which had been vital and alive, was now dead, and the world simply went on. So powerful was the message that Brian had shivered with fear. Now, after his father's death, the fear is absent. Brian is able to accept much more calmly the mystery of death and its place in the scheme of things:

> People were forever born; people forever died, and never were again. Fathers died and sons were born; the prairie was forever, with its wind whispering through the long, dead grasses, through the long and endless silence. Winter came and spring and fall, then summer and winter again; the sun rose and set again, and everything that was once—was again—forever and forever. But for man, the prairie whispered —never—never. For Brian's father—never. (pp. 246-247)

However, the vision does not end there. In his moment of sadness, the tears streaming down his cheeks for the first time since his father's death, Brian thinks of his mother. He fixes upon "the dark well of his mother's loneliness." He turns from his preoccupation with his own feelings outward to others. It is a new start. It is a moment of epiphany, of startling insight. Accompanied by the beauty of the meadow lark's song, he feels a "fierce excitement" within him and starts for home: his response to his vision is a new sense of duty. Consequently, he experiences "a new and warmer relationship with his mother" and becomes "the head of the family." He looks after Bobbie in a way that he had not before. His relationship with his grand-mother becomes closer spiritually. In the two years after his father's death, reflection gives way to action. Mere feeling gives way to a sense of duty. The center of his universe shifts and moves from within himself outward. As a result, his attention is less introverted, less devoted to seeking to recreate the thrill and excitement of earlier visions:

In the two years since, he had seldom thought of the yearning that had harried him as long as he could remember. Fragments of remembrance would return to him from the past: the dimly recollected picture of a dead pigeon, a tailless gopher lying on the prairie, something about a dewdrop . . . Once he had recalled the two-headed calf to Fat and Art; they remembered it, but that was all. (p. 252)

Trying to recapture the old feeling, he goes to see Saint Sammy, but the man's religious ravings serve only to sadden him. Brian has changed. The change is a step toward maturity. The child, preoccupied with his own feelings, has become a young man whose eyes are turned toward society.

The death of Brian's grandmother helps to reveal the characteristics of Brian's new-found maturity. In spite of Brian's intense love for his grandmother, her death does not cause "shocking impact." He accepts it calmly and reflectively. As he confesses to Mr. Digby, it makes him think more and more of the conversation with Milt Palmer, in which Digby and Palmer had discussed the mystery of reality (Chapter 31). Consequently, Brian says to Mr. Digby that he does not think he will get "the feeling" anymore. Digby looks at the boy with new interest, seeing "maturity in spite of the formlessness of childish features, wisdom without years." Brian has experienced, Digby concludes, "Intimations of Immortality."

Digby's phrase is the title of a poem by William Wordsworth. In that poem, Wordsworth recalls his childhood as a time of sensuous joy in the beauty of all things:

There was a time when meadow, grove, and stream,
The earth and every common sight,
        To me did seem
        Apparelled in celestial light,
The glory and the freshness of a dream.

The experience recollected by the poet is startlingly similar to Brian's early, more childish visions out on the prairie or gazing at the spirea leaf. However, as Wordsworth declares, maturity brings change:

99

It is not now as it hath been of yore;—
  Turn wheresoe'er I may,
   By night or day,
The things which I have seen I now can see no more.

In growing up and leaving behind the innocent joy of childhood, the poet becomes aware of the transience of all things. Like Brian when experiencing the intervention of death, the poet asks, "Whither is fled the visionary gleam?" The answer is not gloomy. All things, he learns, are guided by the hand of God; all existence is part of the divine scheme of things. Nature is not indifferent, for nature is part of God's plan, and man is not alone in the world:

Our birth is but a sleep and a forgetting:
The Soul that rises with us, our life's Star,
  Hath had elsewhere its setting,
   And cometh from afar:
  Not in entire forgetfulness,
  And not in utter nakedness,
But trailing clouds of glory do we come
  From God, who is our home:
Heaven lies about us in our infancy!
Shades of the prison-house begin to close
  Upon the growing Boy,
But he beholds the light, and whence it flows,
  He sees it in his joy;
The Youth, who daily farther from the east
  Must travel, still is Nature's priest,
   And by the vision splendid
   Is on his way attended.

Digby is correct. The vision that Brian comes to after his grandmother's death is not unlike the poet's vision. It is a vision founded upon faith in nature's purpose. It is a vision strengthened by acceptance of what is, so questions about meaning no longer torture Brian. He is able to postpone actual answers: "Some day, he thought, perhaps when he was older than he was now, he would know." For now, it is enough to know that, as a human being, he is part of a process that must be accepted. To be human means to enter into the world of experience. To be mature means to accept being human:

> It had something to do with dying; it had something to do with being born. Loving something and being hungry were with it too. He knew that much now. There was the prairie; there was a meadow lark, a baby pigeon, and a calf with two heads. In some haunting way the Ben was part of it. So was Mr. Digby. (p. 299)

Brian has learned something that Milt Palmer was unwilling to accept. It is a lesson best expressed in the terms of the philosopher, Berkeley: that man is an idea in the mind of God; insight means that man has the assurance that his existence is not meaningless. To be human is, as Brian learns, "awful," but it is not hopeless.

In summary, Brian's journey to intellectual and spiritual maturity has taken him through several well-defined stages:

1. A state of innocence
2. A sense of life's mystery (the death of the pigeon)
3. An awareness of judgment (Miss MacDonald's threats)
4. An insight into moral order (the gopher)
5. A vision of imperfection (the calf, the runt and Annie)
6. An experience of the emptiness that death brings (Jappy)
7. An acceptance of duty (his father's death)
8. An assurance of meaning (his grandmother's death)

Social Criticism

There is one other major theme in the novel, and that is the social criticism that forms an intrinsic part of the narrative.

Who Has Seen The Wind has some of the flavor of the writings of Stephen Leacock, Canada's famous humorist, who satirizes small-town life in Ontario. For example, Mitchell's villains are comic caricatures who stimulate amusement. Mrs. Abercrombie, the banker's wife, is a large, imposing woman with an exaggerated sense of her own importance:

By virtue of her rings, the dignity of her husband's work, a trip they had taken to Europe six years before, and a certain insensitivity to what others thought, her social position was unassailable. (p. 46)

Another villain, Mr. Powelly, is presented in a way that emphasizes the vanity and cold inhumanity of the man:

Mr. Powelly was entering, his light, fawn hair brought carefully over the balding front of his head in thin strings that looked as though they had been glued to his pale scalp; his hands were swallowed to the finger-tips in the sleeves of his gown, whose loose arc over his shoulders, as he turned to ascend to the pulpit, reminded Brian of the coloring on a magpie's back. It was an ascetic's face that turned to the congregation, spare and long-jawed; an absent-mindedly indulgent smile, lifting the corners of his wide and almost lipless mouth, made his sharp features speciously benign. (p. 111)

Miss MacDonald, the sadistic primary teacher, is similarly captured with a handful of vivid phrases that expose her insensitive personality:

She was an efficient woman who looked for results; a strapping was fruitless, she felt, unless a child broke down and stood red and sodden-eyed before her; the more hiccoughs and tears, the more effective the punishment.

However, the term "villain," used to describe these three characters, is not employed lightly. They are not simply comic buffoons whose antics end in laughter. They are, in a real sense, representatives of the forces of evil in the town.

The novel can be seen, from one point of view, as a kind of morality play. The characters, for example, fall into two camps. There are the obviously good characters, and there are the obviously evil characters, and the subplots give an account of the struggle between the two. Eventually, as in all morality plays, good triumphs over evil, and although the battles have their comic aspects, the struggle is a grim one, fought over serious matters.

Mrs. Abercrombie, the evil protagonist, is not a harmless woman. Indeed, she is extremely vicious. Early in the book, she is responsible for the departure of the Presbyterian minister, Mr. Hislop. He is a devout man, full of Christian kindness and humility, but he is something of a dreamer and is certainly no politician. He is like the good parson in Chaucer's *Prologue to the Canterbury Tales*—pious, other-worldly and scholarly but, from the point of view of the cynical world, impractical. When Mr. Hislop angers Mrs. Abercrombie with his compassion for the poor, unfortunate Romona, the minister's fate is sealed. With spiteful wickedness she seizes upon a different issue: the use of candles in the church service. Such is her influence that she persuades the church elders to censure the minister, who is broken by the irrational criticism and resigns.

Mrs. Abercrombie triumphs also in her efforts to ostracize the Wong family. Working with her daughter, Mariel, she has the China Kids, as they are called, shunned at school. When they have a birthday party, Mariel is instructed not to attend, and the Wong children are deeply hurt. Later, when Mr. Wong, overcome by despondency at his wife's death, proves to be incapable of looking after Tang and Vooie, Mrs. Abercrombie is a prime influence in having them sent elsewhere to live. This event is a mortal blow to Mr. Wong, who hangs himself. Mrs. Abercrombie's triumph has had tragic consequences that she could not have foreseen.

Her sole defeat occurs when she joins with Mr. Powelly in an attempt to have the Young Ben sent to reform school. Her real target in the dispute is Mr. Digby, who has angered her on two counts: the first in his apparent refusal to support Miss MacDonald's reign of terror; the second in his describing Mariel as lazy. However, she miscalculates the reactions of the other school trustees. Shamed by Miss Thompson's criticisms and unwilling to see both of their teachers leave, they rebel. Mrs. Abercrombie is forced to leave the school board meeting in humiliation.

Mr. Powelly is Mrs. Abercrombie's able ally. He is clearly a narrow-minded bigot, capable of as much wicked behavior as his colleague. The Ben is his target; he is intransigent in his hounding of the Ben. To a degree, Mr. Powelly's course of vengeance is successful—the Ben is jailed. The whole bitter struggle is a vivid revelation of the minister's striking weaknesses: he is a man of colossal egotism and vanity. He was flattered by the Ben's first expressions of new religious faith. He welcomes the sinner so enthusiastically into the fold that it is obvious that he sees the Ben's conversion as a victory bringing glory to him. Consequently, when the new apostle shows so dramatically that he is still a sinner, Mr. Powelly is furious. He has been made to look foolish, an experience he cannot tolerate. He transfers the vendetta to the Ben's son. In his campaign to have the Young Ben prosecuted, his malevolence is even more disgusting. His character is unredeemed by any of the usual Christian virtues.

Miss MacDonald is a minor villain, though a villain none the less. Mrs. O'Connal understands her very well. The teacher is a bitter, frustrated woman who takes false pride in her harsh, uncompromising attitudes. She dominates her classroom in a way that is unnecessary and insensitive. Thus, unlike Digby, she is completely unable to understand the problem of the Young Ben. He is, in the classroom, a center of power of which she becomes afraid. Since she is basically cowardly, she leaves the boy alone. However, when she feels there is no threat to her authority, she wields her own power cruelly. Her treatment of Brian in the incident of the unwashed hands is evidence enough. She terrifies the young boy so that he has nightmares and is ill for two days. Her methods and attitudes ultimately work to her undoing, as they probably had done in her earlier career; she had resigned her previous position after a dispute with her board. Consequently, she is a pathetic villain, lonely and unsuccessful, though the harm she does is incalculable.

The good characters are clearly portrayed and are active in the cause of goodness.

James Digby, the principal of the school, loves the children for whom he is responsible. That love is not merely empty sentimentality. Digby is a fighter. That is why his advice to his embattled friend, Mr. Hislop, is forthright and unequivocal: " 'Fight 'em,' said Digby. 'Get up there and give it to them.' "

Though sensitive and compassionate, he is certainly not weak, as he again indicates in talking to his friend:

> "The trouble with you," said Digby, "is that you're too thin-skinned. You're tender. That's no good if you're a minister—or a schoolteacher. You've got to be tough—good and tough. I'm tough. You're not."
> (p. 55)

Consequently, his goodness is not what Milton called a "cloistered virtue," a virtue that is not tried and tested in action. He constantly visits the Bens, trying to solve the problem of the Young Ben. He deals compassionately with Brian when the boy runs into trouble on his first day at school. He is willing to help pay for the Wongs' groceries. He pays for the gun stolen by the Young Ben. He tries to aid Milt Palmer in his intellectual and philosophical problems. Most of all, he is unyielding in his struggle against Mrs. Abercrombie and Mr. Powelly. For example, he out-argues the clergyman when Powelly applies pressure to have the Young Ben prosecuted. At the end, he is prepared to resign, rather than be a party to sending the Young Ben to reform school.

It is, of course, Miss Thompson who fights most dramatically for good in the novel. Her hour of triumph comes near the end, at the meeting of the school board. There, she embarrasses the chairman with her clear delineation of the hypocrisy involved in the prosecution of the Ben. She also flays Mrs. Abercrombie with evidence of the woman's "insensitive and vindictive persecution" of the Wong children and the wicked "callousness" that led to Wong's death. Mrs. Abercrombie and the board members, she states, have shown her "the heart of darkness." Her speech ended, she offers her resignation and leaves. Even James Digby had not been able to do all of that. It is her speech that leads to the defeat of Mrs. Abercrombie.

The adversaries in the struggle are clearly identified, the cause of the conflict abundantly evident. Compassion, tolerance and ordinary kindness are locked in conflict with insensitivity, bigotry and vindictiveness. Good and evil stand in opposition. W.O. Mitchell's targets are easily known:

—He exposes social and religious bigotry, in the town's callous indifference to the Wong family and Mrs. Abercrombie's campaign against Mr. Hislop.

—He ridicules human vanity, in the portrait of Mrs. Abercrombie's household and Mr. Powelly's rush to convert the Ben.

—He flays moral cowardice, in his picture of the church elders and the fumbling hesitations of the school board.

—He deplores human ignorance, in his account of Sean's failure to persuade others to nurture the land.

—He portrays the depravity of human malice, in the persecution of the Ben family.

—He satirizes human greed in Bent Candy's treatment of Saint Sammy.

There are these targets and more. The novel is not, then, simply the biography of a boy. It is the portrait of a town in which moral corruption thrives. That factor provides, of course, one of the great ironies of the book. A small town, set in the middle of the majestic prairie, with all of its reminders of God's grandeur, might be expected to be an idyllic community in which there was no competitive greed and no moral depravity. Such is not the case. There is abundant evidence in the town of "the heart of darkness." It is an Eden that has fallen into sin.

For that reason, it is worth noting that W.O. Mitchell contrasts the town and the prairie. The town is the source of evil. There, old, enduring values are too often forgotten. Thus, it is appropriate that, when Saint Sammy invokes God's judgment against Bent Candy, the town is considerably damaged. A judgment is delivered against *all* sinners. The town has sinned. In contrast, the prairie goes on through storm and sunshine. Nature has not fallen prey to sin. It is, therefore, appropriate that the novel closes with a beautiful hymn to the prairies.

Imagery

Images are, in a literal sense, word pictures. They are, in this basic sense, vivid portraits of a character, an object or an idea. However, such portraits are more than literal pictures of people, things or ideas. With imagery, the writer repeatedly associates his subject with a whole set of connotations or meanings that take the description far beyond simple representation or actual appearance. The thing then becomes more than simply the thing itself. It becomes, in addition, the bearer of deeper meanings, an image.

An image, then, is a description of something in terms that suggest meanings larger than the description itself. Frequently, though, the image does not appear in isolation. It is repeated, with the same connotations. When that happens, the imagery is usually described as a motif, which is a recurring theme constantly associated with a particular character or idea or object. In the clearest stage, when the relationship between the image and its connotations is undeniably established, the image is usually referred to as a symbol.

Most substantial literature employs imagery, an important technique for the serious writer. In the first place, imagery enriches the writer's context. The prose has more density, a richer weight of significance. In addition, imagery provides a motif that can bind a work together structurally. The imagery becomes a unifying thread running through the fabric of the prose. Finally, the imagery can be another means by which the writer reveals his themes to the reader. By employing imagery, the writer can teach without being "preachy," making significant statements without being obvious.

In *Who Has Seen The Wind*, there are images that enrich the narrative and suggest meanings that are part of the themes of the novel.

The Wind

The wind is, without doubt, the most important image in the book; the title is an indication of that. The words of the title are taken from a lyric by Christina Rossetti (1830-1894), a poet whose work expressed a strong sense of the spiritual

realities lying behind the appearance of profane things. Mitchell
uses the poem as an epigraph to his novel:

> Who has seen the wind?
>   Neither you nor I:
> But when the trees bow down their heads,
>   The wind is passing by.

In these lines, the wind is an invisible force. It cannot be
seen, but its power is apparent. Consequently, stressing these
same qualities of power and invisibility, the wind has been used,
from earliest times, as a symbol of God. The symbol is clearly
appropriate. God, as generations of believers have said, is
powerful, yet invisible. Mitchell makes the association between
the wind and God when in his preface, he says: "Many inter-
preters of the Bible believe the wind to be symbolic of
Godhood." He continues, significantly, by describing his novel
as "the story of a boy and the wind."

The author's statement is a declaration that his novel is
more than the biography of a boy. It is not simply a description
of the stages that mark the passage from childhood to maturity.
Because the story is also of the wind, it is in some sense a story
about God.

W.O. Mitchell has firm precedents for his use of the wind
as a symbol for God. In the *Book of Job*, for example, God
speaks to Job, and God's voice is a whirlwind that reminds the
prophet of His power and His mercy:

> Who hath put wisdom in the inward
> parts? or who hath given understanding
> to the heart?
> Who can number the clouds in wisdom?
> or who can stay the bottles of heaven,
> When the dust groweth into hardness,
> and the clods cleave fast together?
> Wilt thou hunt the prey for the lion?
> or fill the appetite of the young
> lions,
> When they couch in their dens, and
> abide in the covert to lie in wait?

Who provideth for the raven his food?
when his young ones cry unto God, they
wander for lack of meat. (Chapter 38, verses 36-41)

However, the wind in the Bible is not only a symbol of God's power and providence, it is also the image of life. By that is meant life that is inspired, life that is more significant than mere daily existence; it is life in touch with revealed truth. Thus, in *The Acts of the Apostles*, in the New Testament, when the followers of Jesus are visited after his death by the presence of God, "there came a sound from heaven as of a rushing mighty wind, and it filled all the house where they were sitting" (Chapter 2, verse 2). As a result, the apostles, empowered by a revelation of eternal truth, are able to go out and preach the gospel. The wind that came to them was not only a symbol of God's power and love; it was God as revealed truth. In modern literature, the wind is, similarly, an image for God. However, modern literature tends to portray man as an alienated being, and so the wind appears as an image of God that goes unrecognized. Man, in this view, is living a life from which meaning has gone. When meaning, symbolized by wind, does come, it is not recognized or understood. That, for example, is the condition of man described by T.S. Eliot, in *The Waste Land*:

'What is that noise?'
The wind under the door.
'What is that noise now? What is the wind doing?'
Nothing again nothing.

Here, the mighty wind of God is now simply "wind under the door." It has lost its power; it is now "nothing."

W.O. Mitchell uses the wind as a symbol of God in traditional ways. In *Who Has Seen The Wind*, the wind is a symbol of the presence of God, of the truth that God reveals, of the power of God and of the eternity of God.

The wind as the presence of God is seen very early in the novel. In Chapter 1, Brian walks out to the prairie. He had seen the prairie often, but now, significantly, he becomes aware, for the first time in his life, of the sound of the prairie. His new vision of the life of the prairie is accompanied by "the steady wind." He sits down and savors the life around him:

> He picked a pale blue flax-flower at his feet, stared long at the stripings in its shallow throat, then looked up to see a dragonfly hanging on shimmering wings directly in front of him. The gopher squeaked again, and he saw it a few yards away, sitting up, watching him from its pulpit hole. A suave-winged hawk chose that moment to slip its shadow over the face of the prairie. (p. 11)

Brian is seeing things in a new way, and the experience is expressed in terms of wind imagery:

> And all about him was the wind now, a pervasive sighing through great emptiness, unhampered by the buildings of the town, warm and living against his face and in his hair. (p. 11)

It is a "warm and living" presence that Brian encounters. That the wind signals the presence of God seems to be confirmed by Brian's own summing-up of the incident: "God, Brian decided, must like the boy's prairie." There are many other incidents that similarly associate the wind with God's presence. When Brian is discussing God with Mr. Hislop, Brian asserts that the Young Ben has "prairie hair." The prairie boy, he continues, "has wind on him all the time—it gets in his hair." The connection is obvious. The prairie is associated with God's presence; it is his unspoiled kingdom, away from the town. The Young Ben is closely associated with the prairie. Therefore, the Young Ben is to be associated with God. The wind that accompanies the Young Ben's appearances set the seal on that association. Later, reunited with his puppy, which he has been allowed to get back from the Hoffmans, Brian experiences a moment of epiphany. Cradling his dog, he has a strong sense of the goodness and beauty of the world. It is a spiritual experience, full of God's presence:

> The boy was aware that the yard was not still. Every

grass-blade and leaf and flower seemed to be breathing, or perhaps, whispering—something to him—something for him. The puppy's ear was inside out. Within himself, Brian felt a soft explosion of feeling. It was one of completion and of culmination. (p. 60)

Significantly, this experience is accompanied by "a light breeze" that eventually "went whirling out to the prairie." Finally, at the end of the novel, there is a brilliantly poetic passage that is a hymn to the prairie. The vast, unchanging grandeur of the prairie is emphasized. It is seen as a truly eternal kingdom, an appropriate realm for God. The divine presence, seen as the wind, dominates:

The wind turns in silent frenzy upon itself, whirling into a smoking funnel, breathing up topsoil and tumbleweed skeletons to carry them on its spinning way over the prairie, out and out to the far line of the sky. (p. 300)

No less evident is the use of the wind as a symbol of the truth that God reveals. That truth is what Brian seeks throughout the novel. The message is clear but mysterious: man is mortal, and God is eternal. The wind is the carrier of the message. In Digby's thoughts, the prairie wind sings "mortality to every living thing" (p. 31). Later, at a crucial moment in the novel, when Brian is at last able to deal with the fact of his father's death, the wind accompanies the revelation: "All around him the wind was in the grass with a million timeless whisperings." There, on the prairie, he experiences his vision of the mortality of man:

People were forever born; people forever died, and never were again. Fathers died and sons were born; the prairie was forever, with its wind whispering through the long, dead grasses, through the long and endless silence. (p. 246)

Man is born and dies, but the prairie is eternal. The voice of

God speaks in the wind the message that man must learn and, having learned, accept.

Mitchell also uses the wind as a symbol of God's power. This power is not presented as only the power of love. It is the power of Job's whirlwind, which embodies divine wrath and divine judgment. Thus, the wind in the novel is not always gentle; it does not always signal the caress of the divine spirit of love. The wind also chastises and corrects.

For example, at the beginning of the novel, the wind is described as "a long hot gusting that would lift the black topsoil and pile it in barrow pits along the roads, or in deep banks against the fences." The wind, in this instance, is a destructive force, stripping the land of its richness and making the task of the farmer more difficult. It is, in fact, a wind of judgment, punishing the neglect and self-indulgence of the farmers. This is the message that Uncle Sean, "the keeper of the Lord's vineyard," delivers in Chapter 2. He launches into "one of his evangelistic denunciations" against farmers who rob the land of its fertility in the growing season and then depart on vacation in the winter:

> Jist look at her—creased an' pocked an' cracked—no grass to hold the topsoil down! That's what happens when you crop her out an' away fer the winter—then back agin in the spring to scratch at her agin—on agin off agin an' away agin! You wanta travel an' so does she! I seen her travelin' on a first-class ticket by air—she's bin to the Coast with you—a thousand million sections of her—black cloudsa dust blacker than all yer greedy souls—lifted up an' travelin' —travelin' clear to Jesus! (pp. 18-19)

The farmers' problem is of their own making. Sean has the solution. Farmers should plant "in strips acrosst the prevailin' winds"; they should raise livestock, and they should forget their "goddam yella-wheeled cars an' their trips to Washington an' Oregon an' California!" The wind, the messenger of God's judgment, must be heeded.

Certainly, the most dramatic example of the wind as God's judgment occurs in Chapter 28. This episode tells of the destruction of Bent Candy's expensive new barn by a devastating wind that sweeps across the prairie. Saint Sammy has no doubt what the wind is. To him, it is undoubtedly God's wrath visited against Bent Candy for his greed in wanting to possess Sammy's Clydesdale horses:

> The Lord hath blew! He hath blew down the new an' shinin' barn of the fundamental Baptist that hath sinned in His sight! Like He said, 'Sorra an' sighin' hath cometh to Bent Candy!' (p. 272)

The wind as a symbol of the eternity of God is simply another aspect of the wind as revelation. The wind accompanies the revelation of the truth that God, symbolized as the prairie, endures, while man's mortal existence is transitory. Thus, appropriately, the novel opens and closes with an image of the wind. All that has happened between is an illustration of man's mortality. Gerald O'Connal has died and Mrs. MacMurray has died but the prairie is unchanged. It is "the least common denominator of nature," as the first line tells us, and its wind roams "out and out to the far line of the sky," as the final line of the novel tells us. God is the beginning and the ending. God is eternal.

The Prairie

The prairie provides more than a setting for the novel. The prairie is an image related to the themes. It is the realm of the spiritual, as opposed to the town, which is the realm of the profane.

In the first place, the prairie is associated with divine revelation. Brian's first experience of his "special feeling" occurs on the prairie. It takes place in that "great emptiness, unhampered by the buildings of the town." Later, after the baby pigeon's death, Brian suggests to his father that the bird should be buried on the prairie, because "it was just like dirt...like prairie dirt that wasn't alive at all." After the burial, he has a fleeting vision of the limitlessness of the divine. He stands "looking out over the prairie, to its far line where sheet lightning winked up the world's dark rim." In contrast, "pygmy farm buildings stood out momentarily," but are "quickly blotted." Two days later, with an experience that seems to confirm what the prairie revealed, Brian comes to know a sense of "completion" and "culmination." Later still, when he comes upon the decaying remains of the dead gopher, Brian experiences a moment of epiphany:

> Prairie's awful, thought Brian, and in his mind there loomed vaguely fearful images of a still and brooding spirit, a quiescent power unsmiling from everlasting to everlasting to which the coming and passing of the prairie's creatures was but incidental. (pp. 128-129)

In that vast landscape, an aspect of God had been revealed to Brian. Not surprisingly, when Brian faces the most serious crisis of his young life—the death of his father—he experiences revelation of the divine in the prairie, "in the silence that stretched from everlasting to everlasting" (p. 247). His final revelation in the novel, after his grandmother's death, takes place on the prairie again, where the sky "had a depthless softness undetermined by its usual pencil edge" (p. 298).

In the second place, the prairie is an image that proclaims the eternity of God. Men may come and men may go, but the prairie—and God—go on forever. His voice is "the prairie wind that lifted over the edge of the prairie world to sing mortality to every living thing" (p. 31). His presence fills the prairie with a spirit that is "from everlasting to everlasting" (pp. 128-129). The message is announced most clearly after Gerald O'Connal's death:

> People were forever born; people forever died, and never were again. Fathers died and sons were born; the prairie was forever....(p. 246)

The lesson comes, not only in Brian's words, but in the picture of the prairie itself: vast and unmoved, majestic and unchanging. It is, indeed, a picture of an aspect of God.

Finally, the prairie is an image associated with the purity of God. The prairie is constantly associated with a moral impulse that is all-too-frequently stifled in the town. The concept of moral law is, appropriately, conveyed in the two strange characters who are, in effect, symbols of the prairie; the Young Ben and Saint Sammy. Very early, Brian recognizes the connection between the prairie and the Young Ben. On the prairie, Brian "simply accepted the boy's presence...as he had accepted that of the gopher and the hawk and the dragonfly" (p. 12). He declared, "This is your prairie." It is not surprising, then, that Brian associates the Young Ben with his own "special feeling." The association is most explicit in the incident in which Art mistreats the gopher. When the Young Ben punishes Art, Brian experiences a vision of moral law:

> And Brian, quite without any desire to alleviate Art's suffering, shaken by his discovery that the Young Ben was linked in some indefinable way with the magic that visited him often now, was filled with a sense of the justness, the rightness, the completeness of what the Young Ben had done—what he himself would like to have done. (pp. 127-128)

The equation is obvious: the Young Ben equals the prairie; the Young Ben equals justice in action; therefore, the prairie equals moral law. Saint Sammy, the second figure to embody the prairie and its values, is a messenger of divine purity to no less a degree. His telling of the Creation story in his own terms in a vivid portrayal of the essential purity of the prairie:

> An' He got to thinkin', there ain't nobody fer to till this here soil, to one-way her, to drill her, ner to stook the crops, an' pitch the bundles, an' thrash her, when she's ripe fer thrashin', so He took Him some top-soil—made her into the shape of a man—breathed down into the nose with the breatha life.
> That was Adam. He was a man.
> He set him down ontuh a section to the east in the districka Eden—good land—lotsa water.
> The Lord stood back, an' He looked at what He done insidea one week an' she suited Him fine. (p. 197)

The inference is obvious. The prairie is the garden of Eden, pure and unspoiled. God's prairie hermit, living in a piano box on the prairie, announces the message unequivocally. W.O. Mitchell has used the prairie image in *Who Has Seen The Wind* in much the same way as the desert image is used in the Bible. There, the desert is seen as spiritual purity, far different from the immorality and materialism of the towns. When John the Baptist appeared to preach the need for spiritual cleansing, his home was the desert; he avoided the cities and towns. Similarly, when Jesus began his mission, he went into the desert to fast and pray. In the desert, he was tempted by urban dreams of power and wealth, but he returned to the towns to preach against greed and avarice and all the temptations of the material world.

The Town

In contrast to the image of the prairie in the novel is the image of the town. Saint Sammy provides the most explicit judgment of the town's moral decay:

> Sammy's arm with its hand clawed, lifted, and pointed out the town low on the horizon. "Fer they have played the harlot an' the fornicator in the sighta the Lord!" His old voice trembled, thinned, and clutched at a higher pitch. "An' there is sorra an' sighin' over the facea the prairie—herb an' the seed thereoff thirsteth after the water which don't cometh!" (p. 196)

Of course, Sammy is not a very reliable witness. Of course, he is, in some ways, a comic figure. Even Brian is sceptical of Saint Sammy's message:

> It would be so bad, Brian thought, if a person knew, or even knew what it was that he wanted to know. Listening to Saint Sammy, he had been carried away by the fervor of his words; he had felt for a while that he was closer, but it couldn't be right. Saint Sammy was crazy, crazy as a cut calf, Uncle Sean had said. A thing couldn't come closer through a crazy man gone crazy from the prairie. Who cared about anybody liv-

ing in a piano box on the bald-headed prairie? (pp. 198-99)

However, Sammy's judgment has to be considered in the light of the facts, which are clear:

—The religious faith of the town is seen to have a weak spiritual base. The Presbyterian church evicted its pious minister, Mr. Hislop, and welcomed Mr. Powelly, who spends most of his energy in a crusade of revenge against the Ben. The Baptist church is not blessed any differently. Its leading deacon is Bent Candy, whose greed drives him to try to rob Saint Sammy of his beloved horses.

—The bigotry of Mrs. Abercrombie led to the destruction of the Wong family and the suicide of Mr. Wong.

—The hypocrisy of Judge Mortimer caused the imprisoning of the Ben, for a crime in which many of the town's leading citizens were involved.

—The ignorance and irresponsibility of Mr. Abercrombie frustrated Sean O'Connal's efforts to solve prairie problems, because the banker would not lend money for Sean's projects.

—The avaricious self-interest of Bent Candy, described as the "profaner of almost a township of flat loam," also blocks Sean's schemes for the responsible use of prairie land.

The indictment is clear and could be extended. There is too little Christian virtue in the town. It deserves the judgment it receives in the same punishing wind that destroys Bent Candy's barn.

However, the town is not only an image of moral corruption: it is also an image of mortality. Thus, its insignificance is often stressed in contrast with the permanence of the prairie. For example, when Brian's vision comes in its most complete form in the last chapter, there is a description of the town that is quite different from any description of the prairie. The town is "dim—gray and low upon the horizon," lying "not real, swathed in bodiless mist—quite sunless in the rest of the dazzling prairie." Clearly, if the prairie stands for the eternity of God and for the immortality of his presence, the town is a no less powerful image of the insignificance of man's works.

117

In conclusion, it should be emphasized that there are three major sets of images in the novel: the wind, the prairie and the town. They provide a dramatic statement of the relationship between the two major realities in the novel: God and man. It is that relationship that becomes a major focus of Brian's quest: it is that relationship that brings him some small sense of completion.

Selected Criticisms

D.G. Jones

The struggle between a garrison culture and the land provides the basic pattern for W.O. Mitchell's *Who Has Seen The Wind*. Here the struggle between an authentic and an inauthentic way of life is dramatized as a struggle between the power elite of a small prairie town and the varied assortment of friends and mentors of the young boy, Brian O'Connal, all of whom tend to be associated with the land, with the life of the open prairie and, above all, with the prairie wind. Mrs. Abercrombie, the banker's wife, and the Rev. Mr. Powelly of the Presbyterian church represent the official culture of the town. In their opposition to the Bens and to the school principal, Mr. Digby, they reveal at length the essential hypocrisy and the final sterility of their attitude. Living outside town on the open prairie, the Bens embody the apparently amoral, animal vitality of nature. The Young Ben, completely indifferent to anything that is to be learned in school, is almost wholly identified with the life of the prairie, its gophers, grasshoppers, wind and grass. As Brian observes, he always has the wind on his hair. The Ben keeps the semblance of a farm, does odd jobs, and brews moonshine in a still which he hides in his manure pile. The opposition to the Bens on the part of Mrs. Abercrombie and the Rev. Mr. Powelly is clearly an opposition to the land.

> *Butterfly on Rock, A Study of Themes and Images in Canadian Literature*. University of Toronto Press, 1970.

Robin Mathews

The novel is a comedy. It closes with the forces of light routing the forces of darkness. Mrs. Abercrombie resigns from the school board. Digby and Miss Thompson are about to marry. Brian's future is apparently assured as a dirt doctor. The Young Ben is saved from "an institute of correction." He fades away from the closing parts of the novel almost unnoticed, for he has served his purpose.

The novel is a comedy which presents a consideration of justice at a number of interlocking and interdependent levels. It puts natural justice, social justice, and divine justice into relation, and seeks, humorously, in the words of John Milton in *Paradise Lost*, to "justify the ways of God to men," which means to show the justice of God's ways to men.

Canadian Literature, Surrender or Revolution.
Steel Rail Educational Publishing. Toronto, 1978.

W.H. New

In introducing characters such as the Young Ben or Saint Sammy, who are in some ways the most vividly drawn of all the people in the book, Mitchell runs the danger of letting his focus shift from the central development. Such a shift occurs in *The Kite* and weakens that book, but in *Who Has Seen The Wind*, the focus is fortunately sustained, and because of this, the author achieves a remarkable insight into the operation of his central character's mind. Though much of this novel deals with characters other than Brian O'Connal, Brian's growth to responsibility always remains central, and the various successful and unsuccessful adaptations that the minor characters make in their respective situations of conflict, reflect upon this central growth. Svarich, for example, fails to accept his Ukrainian identity; Hislop fails to accept the existence of opposition in his church and merely resigns. Sean, Digby and Miss Thompson, however, come to take responsible positions in their own spheres; they act positively to solve the conflict in which they find themselves, and yet they are able at the same time to accept what they cannot control. Brian, therefore, has both examples before him. Also before him are the vividly-drawn Saint Sammy and Young Ben with their strange adaptive abilities, but even they remain minor figures, because they, too, serve to contribute an understanding of the emotional sensitivity of Brian himself.

Articulating West, Essays on Purpose and
Form in Modern Canadian Literature.
New Press. Toronto, 1972.

120

Review Questions

1. Trace the appearances of the wind imagery in the novel, and explain their relation to the title.

2. Trace the development of Brian's "feeling" throughout the novel. What is the final insight that he comes to understand?

3. Examine the intellectual views of: (a) Mr. Digby (b) Milt Palmer (c) Mr. Hislop.

4. Select one comic scene from the novel and explain the techniques that create the humor.

5. Write an essay on the challenges and frustrations of being a teacher in a small prairie town.

6. Give an account of life in the O'Connal family.

7. Write a biography of Mrs. MacMurray, including her homesteading days.

8. Give an account of social satire in the novel.

9. Research prairie farming problems, and evaluate Sean's ideas in the light of your research.

10. Discuss Mitchell's view of formal religion, as it is seen in the novel.

Bibliography

Jones, Douglas G. *Butterfly on Rock: A Study of Themes and Images in Canadian Literature.* Toronto: University of Toronto Press, 1970.

Klinck, Carl F. (ed.) *Literary History of Canada.* Toronto: University of Toronto Press, 1977.

Mathews, Robin. *Canadian Literature: Surrender or Revolution.* Toronto: Steel Rail Educational Publishing, 1978.

Pacey, Desmond. *Creative Writing in Canada.* Toronto: Ryerson Press, 1961.

Stephens, Donald (ed.). *Writers of the Prairies.* Vancouver: University of British Columbia Press, 1973.

Thomas, Clara. *Our Nature — Our Voices: A Guidebook to English-Canadian Literature.* Toronto: New Press, 1972.

Waterston, Elizabeth. *Survey: A Short History of Canadian Literature.* Toronto: Methuen, 1973.